Were Native Americans the Victims of Genocide?

David M. Haugen

ReferencePoint Press®

San Diego, CA

About the Author
David M. Haugen is a writer, editor, and educator living in Kentucky.

For more information, contact:
ReferencePoint Press, Inc.
PO Box 27779
San Diego, CA 92198
www. ReferencePointPress.com

LIBRARY OF CONGRESS CATALOGING-IN-PUBLICATION DATA

Name: Haugen, David M., 1969– author.
Title: Were Native Americans the Victims of Genocide?/by David M. Haugen.
Description: San Diego, CA: ReferencePoint Press, Inc., [2018] | Includes
    bibliographical references and index.
Identifiers: LCCN 2017037143 (print) | LCCN 2017037777 (ebook) | ISBN
    9781682822920 (eBook) | ISBN 9781682822913 (hardback)
Subjects: LCSH: Indians of North America—Colonization—Juvenile literature.
    | Indians, Treatment of—North America—History—Juvenile literature. |
    Indians of North America—Violence against—Juvenile literature. | Indians
    of North America—Wars—Juvenile literature. | Genocide—United
    States—History—Juvenile literature. | United States—Race
    relations—History.
Classification: LCC E77 (ebook) | LCC E77 .H38 2018 (print) | DDC
    970.004/97—dc23
LC record available at https://lccn.loc.gov/2017037143

CONTENTS

Important Events   4

Introduction   6
A Question of Intent

Chapter One   11
The Arrival of the Europeans

Chapter Two   23
Colonial Settlement

Chapter Three   34
The Expansion West

Chapter Four   45
Removal, Relocation, and Assimilation

Chapter Five   57
The Western Indian Wars

Source Notes   68

For Further Research   73

Index   76

Picture Credits   80

1532
Francisco Pizarro sets out to conquer the Incan Empire in Peru, a feat he will accomplish with guns, cannons, and horses.

1784
A year after the end of the American Revolution, the Treaty of Fort Stanwix forces the Iroquois to give up their land in the Ohio River valley, allowing for more westward expansion into Pennsylvania.

1779
George Washington orders General John Sullivan and four brigades of colonial regulars to march into Iroquois territory to destroy their ability to wage war.

1492
Christopher Columbus reaches the New World and establishes a colony on the Caribbean island of Hispaniola (now Haiti and the Dominican Republic).

1607
England's Virginia Company founds Jamestown in modern-day Virginia. It is the first permanent English settlement in the New World.

1400   1500   1600   1700   1800

1776
The thirteen colonies in America declare their independence from Great Britain. Many Native tribes join the British to fight the colonists, who are still pushing westward.

1519
Spanish conquistador Hernán Cortés begins his conquest of the Aztec Empire in Mexico.

1620
Puritan separatists from England establish Plymouth Colony in Massachusetts. The Puritans initially have peaceful relations with the nearby tribes, but expansion of the colony leads to conflict and war.

1866
The Oglala Lakota chief Red Cloud begins a war over land rights and settlement in Sioux territory. The Lakota, northern Cheyenne, and northern Arapaho unite and successfully pin down the US Army in the region.

1890
The massacre of Indians at Wounded Knee, South Dakota, signals the end of major battles in the Indian Wars in the western United States.

1830
Congress passes the Indian Removal Act, targeting the Cherokee, Chickasaw, Choctaw, Creek (modern-day Muscogee), and Seminole for resettlement west of the Mississippi. The Choctaw are the first tribe to be relocated, suffering hardship and death along what will eventually be called the Trail of Tears.

1869
William Tecumseh Sherman is appointed commanding general of the US Army. His ruthless tactics—which include killing buffalo herds and sacking Native villages—end many conflicts with Indians in the West, pushing them back onto shrinking reservations.

1900
According to the US Census, only about 230,000 Native Americans live in the entire United States and its continental territories (excluding Alaska and Hawaii). The average estimate of Native people living in North America before European contact is 8 million.

1820 **1840** **1860** **1880** **1900**

1848
Gold is discovered at Sutter's Mill in California, kicking off the California Gold Rush.

1887
Congress passes the Dawes Act, which gave the government the power to break up tribal land and reapportion it into lots owned by individuals rather than whole tribes.

1829
Andrew Jackson becomes president and begins a broad policy of removing Indian tribes from the eastern United States and resettling them onto land acquired through the Louisiana Purchase of 1803.

1876
A combined force of Lakota, Cheyenne, and Arapaho warriors, led by Crazy Horse and Sitting Bull, defeat General George Armstrong Custer at the Battle of the Little Bighorn.

1864
Colorado volunteers led by Colonel John Chivington stage the Sand Creek Massacre against a camp of Arapaho and Cheyenne who were negotiating for peace.

1838
The Potawatomi, the last of the Great Lakes tribes to be resettled, are forced out of the region by militia units.

A Question of Intent

The term *genocide* became part of modern language after World War II. It was then that the United Nations looked to define the purposeful, systematic evil of Adolf Hitler's Final Solution to the "Jewish problem" in Europe. The intent of the term's creation was to identify and categorize a criminal action, the murder (*cide*) of a race or tribe (*genos*). The word was used in the Allied courts that tried several Nazi leaders, but it did not become a recognized criminal offense until it entered into international law with the passing of the Convention on the Prevention and Punishment of the Crime of Genocide in 1948. Article II of that convention defines genocide as certain acts "committed with intent to destroy, in whole or in part, a national, ethnical, racial or religious group."[1] These include outright killing, removing children from one group to another, or reducing the quality of life of a target group in order to bring about its destruction. The United Nations utilized the convention in the 1990s to indict contemporary war criminals in Bosnia and Rwanda and in the early 2000s to prosecute members of Pol Pot's murderous regime in Cambodia during the 1970s.

Native American Genocide?

Many historians and activists in the United States believe the term should also be used to define the tragedies visited upon the indigenous peoples in the Americas from the fifteenth century through modern times. To them the activities of the Spanish, English, Dutch, and to some extent French explorers and colonists who came to the New World resulted in the death, injury, or mental anguish of numerous individuals; the removal of indigenous people from their homelands; and in some instances, the eradication of whole tribes. In her 2014 book *An Indigenous*

6

Peoples' History of the United States, author and educator Roxanne Dunbar-Ortiz declares that the process of colonization in the United States brought to bear many tools to destroy Native American lifestyles, communities, and individuals. She writes, "From the colonial period through the founding of the United States and continuing in the twenty-first century, this has entailed torture, terror, sexual abuse, massacres, systematic military occupations, removals of Indigenous peoples from their ancestral territories, and removals of Indigenous children to military-like boarding schools." She believes *genocide* is an apt term to define the intent of these actions and that "the absence of even the slightest note of regret or tragedy in the annual celebration of the US independence betrays a deep disconnect in the consciousness of US Americans."[2]

Dunbar-Ortiz's "deep disconnect" suggests that modern Americans are ignorant of—or worse, willfully ignore—the destruction of Native people that accompanied the settling, founding, and building of the nation. But whether this devastation amounts to genocide—a criminal offense—is still debated because some critics resist the notion that colonials set out to eradicate Native Americans. Many point out that European diseases proved to be the most effective killer of Native populations, and men like Christopher Columbus, who first brought disease to the New World, had no idea what germs were or that the Native Americans would lack resistance to them. Educator and entrepreneur Rod D. Martin insists that European diseases were regrettable but not an act of genocide, "[for] if one posits this, who exactly should we hold accountable? Europeans did not even know bacteria existed (and wouldn't know they were linked to disease for another four hundred years)."[3] Others note that the mission of the Spanish, Portuguese, and others who first set up outposts in the Americas was never to eliminate the Native peoples. After all, Christian missionaries spent great effort attempting to win new converts from the pagan tribes in hopes of spreading God's word.

> "The absence of even the slightest note of regret or tragedy in the annual celebration of the US independence betrays a deep disconnect in the consciousness of US Americans."[2]
>
> —Author and educator Roxanne Dunbar-Ortiz

Cheyenne move through the Great Plains in the late nineteenth century. Whether the treatment of Native Americans by Europeans during colonization amounts to genocide is still debated today.

An American Holocaust

American Indian studies professor Ward Churchill insists that apologists for European colonists are wrong to argue that the Spanish, English, and others had no intention of destroying the Native populations. Churchill likens Columbus's interactions with the Taino tribes he encountered in the Caribbean to the Nazi campaign to rid Europe of the Jews. In Churchill's view, Columbus "instituted policies of enslavement . . . and systematic extermination against the native Taino population." The near destruction of the islanders, he claims, "constitutes an attrition of population *in real numbers* every bit as great as the toll of twelve to fifteen million—about half of them Jewish—most commonly attributed to [the death camps of Nazi Germany]."[4] He maintains that the percentage of Taino destroyed alone was even greater than that of European Jewry during the Holocaust of World War II.

Not everyone agrees with the comparison, however. As former *Newsweek* editor Kenneth Auchincloss argues, the justification for labeling the early Spanish practices as genocide relies on a modern understanding of the term, one that is informed by the relatively recent Jewish Holocaust and the contemporary concerns for indigenous peoples' rights and the environment. Auchincloss writes, "For all sorts of reasons, minority populations, non-European cultures and tropical forests enjoy a lot of sympathy these days. If these are your primary concerns, it's fairly easy to paint Columbus and the early explorers as people who oppressed the local residents, smashed alien civilizations and chopped down a lot of trees. It's a damning portrait. But it also leaves a lot out." What is left out, Auchincloss says, is that the motivations for the exploration of the New World were often driven by scientific curiosity, a desire to spread faith, and a feeling that the expansion of Western civilization was in part Europe's destiny. He claims, "The impulses that lay behind the voyage to the New World were by no means so uniformly nasty as they are sometimes portrayed."[5]

> "It's fairly easy to paint Columbus and the early explorers as people who oppressed the local residents, smashed alien civilizations and chopped down a lot of trees. It's a damning portrait. But it also leaves a lot out."[5]
>
> —Former *Newsweek* editor Kenneth Auchincloss

An Ongoing Debate

However, Auchincloss and other critics do not shy away from pointing out that European destiny came at the expense of those who were clearly not part of it. Martin argues that the Native Americans were not passive in the face of colonialism but simply did not prevail. He notes that many did take up arms and resist. But Martin asserts that it is wrong to think of the Indians as unified in their struggle; they fought often against each other for land and game as well as against the Europeans. But of their contest against the Europeans and their foreign diseases, he writes, "The Indians—a nebulous term encompassing countless separate tribes who did not then identify with one another in any way—lost. But they fought. They weren't slaughtered by the whites: they were slaughtered by the germs. And for most of four hundred years after, they held their own, extremely well."[6]

Whether these types of arguments will carry any weight with a nation that is constantly being asked to reevaluate its past in order to address the present is yet to be determined. And even if America admits to the genocide of Native people, no one is sure what would come of this admission. As Auchincloss states, "It was just history, like all the rest of history, and it happened not in an instant but over an extremely long stretch of time. And thankfully, the American nation that rose in the Indians' place not only includes them, but has attained to values and compassion that today make discussions like this one possible."[7]

However, some argue that much of what passes as American history overlooks the sinister—even reprehensible—acts of the nation to favor tales of glory, destiny, and expansion. Dunbar-Ortiz remarks, "Those who seek history with an upbeat ending, a history of redemption and reconciliation, may look around and observe that such a conclusion is not visible, not even in utopian dreams of a better society."[8] To her and others, the country needs to become more familiar with the destruction of Native peoples so that future generations recognize that America was not settled, but colonized, by white Europeans and that the consequences of that colonization continue to impact the nation, its politics, and its social fabric today.

CHAPTER ONE

The Arrival of the Europeans

On October 12, 1492, after two and a half months of navigating three ships westward across the southern Atlantic Ocean, the explorer Christopher Columbus spied unfamiliar islands on the horizon. Convinced that he had sailed his small fleet around the world and arrived in Asia, Columbus eagerly began claiming the lands he "found" for King Ferdinand and Queen Isabella of Spain. These monarchs were the only European rulers willing to support and outfit Columbus, an Italian by birth, in the hopes that the riches of the Far East would flow into their royal coffers. They promised Columbus that he would be governor of all the new lands he could claim or conquer. They also agreed to give him a share of the profits from the valuable ocean trade route his voyage would establish.

Suitably motivated, Columbus first made landfall on what is now the Bahamas on October 14 and then, continuing his exploration, made several more stops in present-day Cuba and Hispaniola (the island that at present is home to the Dominican Republic and Haiti). At the time, no other European had set foot on these Caribbean islands, so Columbus felt justified in claiming each in turn. In a 1493 letter to Ferdinand and Isabella, he wrote, "I took possession of all of them for our most fortunate King by making public proclamation and unfurling his standard [flag], no one making any resistance."[9] No one can be certain where Columbus thought he had landed or why he felt justified in claiming the islands, but it is likely that Columbus initially believed the new territories were all part of the Indies, a general term at the time for the various lands that make up southern and eastern Asia. Consequently, he referred to the islanders whom he encountered as "Indians."

Columbus Encounters the People of the New World

Columbus's first impression of these unresisting Native people was that they were easily cowed. Columbus informed his sovereigns that the tribes lacked iron to make strong weapons, but he was doubtful they would have had the spirit to use such arms anyway. He recalled in the letter:

> It has often happened, when I have sent two or three of my men to some of their villages to speak with the inhabitants, that a crowd of Indians has sallied forth; but when they saw our men approaching, they speedily took to flight, parents abandoning children, and children their parents. This happened not because any loss or injury had been inflicted upon any of them. On the contrary I gave whatever I had, cloth and many other things, to whomsoever I approached, or with whom I could get speech, without any return being made to me; but they are by nature fearful and timid.[10]

The Taino of the Bahamas, Cuba, and Hispaniola were naturally cautious, for they had never seen European sailing vessels or the clothing and guns that the sailors possessed. However, curiosity and congeniality must have overcome their concerns, because Columbus wrote of his peaceful negotiations with the tribes. In his letter Columbus informed Ferdinand and Isabella that he forbade his men from trading worthless trinkets for gold and cotton—two items the Europeans desired—because he considered the exchange unjust. Though he may have been unwilling to cheat the Native people, Columbus had other objectives in mind. He wrote of how he hoped to convert the tribes to Christianity and to turn the Native people into loyal subjects of the crown. In addition, Columbus stated that he worked to establish good relations with the Native people "that they might be eager to search for and gather and give to us what they abound in and we greatly need."[11]

To establish good relations, though, Columbus admitted that he took several tribesmen by force aboard his ships to act as

In 1492 explorer Christopher Columbus arrives in the New World—on what is now the Bahamas—and claims the land for the king and queen of Spain.

guides and intermediaries who could entice wary Native people to come out of hiding. He also seized seven individuals from the first village he encountered so that he could take them back to Spain and teach them Spanish. Columbus does not mention any ill treatment of the islanders he abducted or of those with whom he transacted ashore. In his diaries, though, he mentioned that he could easily overpower the Taino, "for with fifty men they can all be subjugated and made to do what is required of them."[12] But Columbus was looking for trade, not war. His goal was to find a shorter trade route to the markets of the Far East and claim everything along that route for Spain. There is no evidence that he initially intended to subdue or devastate the Native populations.

> "With fifty men [the Taino] can all be subjugated and made to do what is required of them."[12]
>
> —Christopher Columbus

However, some modern critics argue that Columbus's opinion of the people he encountered was condescending and eventually led to their enslavement and destruction. Like most of the early explorers who followed, Columbus did not see the Native people as equal to Europeans. Though he was impressed by their good nature and generous spirit, he considered them lost souls who walked naked through a heathen paradise. He noted how the tribes were "very ready and prone"[13] to accept Christianity, and he believed it was his duty and the obligation of Spain to speed their conversion to the faith. Columbus also recognized that these potential converts were a means to an end, for their gold jewelry and trinkets and their stories of fabled treasures suggested that these islands were ripe not only for trade but plunder. In the conclusion to his aforementioned letter, he clarified the value of the islanders by affirming to the king and queen, "Let us be glad not only for the exaltation of our faith, but also for the increase of temporal prosperity, in which not only Spain but all Christendom is about to share."[14]

The Quest for Wealth

American studies professor David E. Stannard claims Columbus's willingness to forcefully take Native Americans aboard his ships was rooted in a European mind-set that prized wealth and condoned violence. Stannard argues that the fifteenth century had witnessed officially sanctioned violence in the form of wars, witch hunts, religious persecutions, and the torture of heretics. Stannard notes that in the years Columbus was voyaging, the Spanish Inquisition (which began in 1478) was still active, seeking to rid the land of heresy and convert nonbelievers. Executions were common and exemplified the absolute power of monarchs and the Church. Still, many in the lower classes attended them as alluring spectacle. As *Smithsonian* author Timothy Foote states of the fifteenth century, "Few ages, except our own . . . had more morbid fascination with torment, killing and death, or more . . . action to satisfy it."[15] For these reasons, Stannard and others believe violence was so ingrained in late medieval society that Columbus would not have been averse to using it to achieve his goals.

In addition, slavery was a common practice in Spain and the rest of Europe during Columbus's era. Most slaves came from eastern Europe and the Middle East, but Columbus suggested in

Celebrating Columbus Day

On the second Monday in October, Americans observe Columbus Day. The national holiday celebrates Christopher Columbus's landing in the Americas, opening the continents to European exploration. But not everyone agrees that the man is worth honoring. In recent times, critics of Columbus have demanded his holiday be removed from the federal roster. They cite Columbus's poor treatment of the Native people in the Caribbean and his efforts to sell many of them into slavery as grounds for dismissing any celebration of the man or his deeds. For example, the Reverend David Felten states, "Any claim that one might have to Columbus having been a noble explorer worth honoring with a Federal holiday is eclipsed by the reality of the inhumanity he visited upon his fellow human beings."

Felten is not alone. Various Native American groups have long called for a reconsideration of the holiday, and progressive political commentators have written numerous articles that expose to the public the atrocities committed by the explorer. Some cities have even gone so far as to launch their own holidays to coincide with Columbus Day; these new holidays celebrate indigenous people, not the so-called discovery of America.

However, the day has its defenders. The Order Sons of Italy in America, for one, maintains that Americans should observe Columbus Day because "the arrival of Columbus in 1492 marks the beginning of recorded history in America, [and] Columbus Day celebrates the beginning of cultural exchange between America and Europe."

Reverend David Felten, "Taking the Columbus Out of Columbus Day," *The Blog, Huffington Post*, October 13, 2014. www.huffingtonpost.com.

Order Sons of Italy in America, "Why We Should Celebrate Columbus Day." www.osia.org.

his writings that he had spent some time sailing under the Portuguese flag while engaged in the slave trade along the West African coast. The Christian Church even condoned slavery, and with this sanction and his own experience with slave trading, it is likely that Columbus felt no shame in forcefully taking indigenous Caribbean people aboard his vessels.

Finally, there is the matter of spoils. Columbus's venture was not driven by a desire to explore but rather by economic obligations. Silks, spices, perfumes, and drugs were highly sought after by Europe's wealthy class, but what they wanted most was more wealth. Stannard writes that the rich in western Europe "hungered after gold and silver"[16] because the Crusades in the Middle East had shown them what could be purchased or plundered from that region and farther east. Ferdinand was no different than other Western monarchs who were drawn to the wealth and treasures of the East, and he only agreed to supply Columbus because he expected a return on his investment. Columbus understood that he needed to repay his sovereign's investment, but he also anticipated turning a profit of his own from his percentage of the loot, as Ferdinand had promised. He knew that opening a trade route across the Atlantic would benefit Spain as well other Western kingdoms and therefore pay dividends through his own share in the haul. And he knew that gold, over all other treasures, would be the most profitable find.

> "Few ages, except our own . . . had more morbid fascination with torment, killing and death, or more . . . action to satisfy it."[15]
>
> —*Smithsonian* author Timothy Foote

These attitudes may have indeed influenced Columbus's treatment of the Native populations. On his return leg to Spain, he had perhaps twenty-five captured Native people on board whom he planned to display to the Spanish court. Stannard claims that only roughly a half dozen survived the voyage, and "only two were alive six months later."[17] In addition to the Caribbean people he brought back, he did manage to return with a pineapple, a tobacco plant, a turkey, and some gold. His passionate letter to Ferdinand and Isabella coupled with the few prizes on display earned him a second voyage with a much larg-

Spanish conquistadors begin enslaving Native peoples who resist their rule. Slavery and the introduction of European diseases decimated indigenous populations.

er fleet (seventeen ships) and twelve hundred men. Columbus still believed he could find a passage to China if he explored a bit farther west of the islands.

A Legacy of Submission and Slavery Begins

Setting sail in 1493, he touched several islands of the Lesser Antilles and eventually found himself back in Hispaniola. Although his sovereigns asked him to maintain friendly relations with the Native people while colonizing the islands, Columbus had other ideas. Unable to locate Asia or any significant source of gold—and realizing that pineapples and turkeys would not bring profits—he sent a letter to Spain proposing that some of the more aggressive islanders be captured as slaves. Columbus targeted those who were enemies of the tribes that he had befriended on his first voyage. He also aimed to rid himself of all Native Americans who resisted his rule on Hispaniola. The crown refused Columbus's petition, but he ignored the king and queen's wishes and captured between twelve hundred and sixteen hundred Taino to sell into slavery in Europe. He packed five hundred of these individuals into the holds of ships and sent them as presents to Isabella. Appalled by the gesture, the queen spent some time freeing the roughly two hundred who had survived the voyage.

Those Native people who never made it off Columbus's ships likely perished from being confined in a closed space with a foreign crew that carried foreign germs. For along with importing the concept of slavery to the New World, the Europeans brought in unfamiliar diseases to which the Native Americans had no resistance.

Forcing Native People to Submit to God and King

In *A Short Account of the Destruction of the Indies* (written in 1542), the Spanish Dominican friar Bartolomé de las Casas reveals the hypocrisy of the Spaniards who tried to force the Native people of Central America to accept Christianity and foreign rule.

> Great and Injurious was the blindness of those [who] praesided over the Indians; as to the Conversion and Salvation of this People: for they denyed in Effect what they in their flourishing Discourse pretended to, and declar'd with their Tongue what they contradicted in their Heart; for it came to this pass, that the Indians should be commanded on the penalty of a bloody War, Death, and perpetual Bondage, to embrace the Christian Faith, and submit to the Obedience of the Spanish King; as if the Son of God, who suffered Death for the Redemption of all Mankind, had enacted a Law, when he pronounced these words, Go and teach all Nations that Infidels, living peaceably and quietly in their Hereditary Native Country, should be impos'd upon pain of Confiscation of all their Chattels, Lands, Liberty, Wives, Children, and Death itself, without any precedent instruction to Confess and Acknowledge the true God, and subject themselves to a King, whom they never saw, or heard mention'd before; and whose Messengers behav'd themselves toward them with such Inhumanity and Cruelty as they had done hitherto. Which is certainly a most foppish and absurd way of Proceeding, and merits nothing but Scandal, Derision, nay Hell itself.

Bartolomé de las Casas, *A Short Account of the Destruction of the Indies*. Project Gutenberg e-book, 2007. www.gutenberg.org.

A short time after making landfall during the second voyage, a third of Columbus's crew was ravaged by an unnamed sickness. Some pathologists believe it was a swine flu variant, but whatever the origin, the Native Americans had never experienced such an epidemic. Fernández de Oviedo y Valdés, a fifteenth-century historian of the New World, claimed, "All through the land the Indians lay dead everywhere. The stench was great and pestiferous."[18] Having lived with plagues and epidemics, the Europeans could weather the diseases. They recovered and set about searching for gold, crushing all the now weakened Native populations that dared to resist handing over food, women, and loot.

> "All through the land the Indians lay dead everywhere. The stench was great and pestiferous."[18]
>
> —Fifteenth-century historian Fernández de Oviedo y Valdés

Over the next several years, the Native population decreased rapidly. Author and radio host Thom Hartmann writes that "some scholars place the population of Haiti/Hispaniola . . . at around 1.5 to 3 million people [prior to 1492]. By 1496, it was down to 1.1 million, according to a census done by Bartholomew Columbus."[19] (Bartholomew was Christopher's younger brother and subsequent governor of the Spanish colony on Hispaniola.) Within another two decades, that number was twelve hundred, Hartmann reports, and it continued to dwindle until no Taino remained in 1555, roughly fifty years after Columbus's death.

The Continuing Spanish Mission in the New World

The Spanish explorers who followed Columbus were equally determined to find the riches of the New World. By the early sixteenth century, it was evident that the Caribbean islands as well as the coasts of Central and South America were indeed unexplored territories and not the fringes of Far Eastern nations. Rumors and legends passed from sailors to traders to merchants, and aristocrats convinced the greedy and the curious that Columbus had simply not explored far enough or taken advantage of the existing opportunities. Author Kirkpatrick Sale remarks that subsequent explorers were easily satisfied that these lands "were endowed with unexpected riches available for the taking (gold and silver, dye-wood and codfish, not to mention cocoa, turkeys, and other exotica), and they were populated by naked heathens whom armed Christians could easily displace."[20] Thus, throughout the 1500s the Spanish and then the Portuguese made the journey across the Atlantic to marvel at the New World. Missionaries came to save the souls of the Native Americans, but the majority had wealth on their minds.

Some of the new foreigners followed the practices that Columbus had already instituted. For example, as governor of the new territories, Columbus had divided the Native populations up into workforces that were then given to loyal Spaniards. Some groups were then forced to work in mines, digging for gold, silver, or gemstones. Others were confined to plantations, where they labored to supply cash crops. Many of the workers toiled ceaselessly and died from exhaustion, beatings, and starvation. "In the face of utter hopelessness," Stannard says, "the Indians began simply surrendering their lives. Some committed suicide. Many refused to have children, recognizing that their offspring, even if they successfully endured the Spanish cruelties, would only become slaves themselves."[21]

> "In the face of utter hopelessness, the Indians began simply surrendering their lives."[21]
>
> —Historian David E. Stannard

The Conquistadors' Hunt for Gold

The most ambitious of the Spaniards, though, were not content with setting up mines and plantations. Men like Hernán Cortés and Francisco Pizarro ventured into the vast lands to the west of the island chains. Cortés explored present-day Mexico; Pizarro traveled through Peru and Chile. Both encountered advanced civilizations that resisted the claims and actions of the intruders. This did not deter these men—known today as conquistadors—who were intent on getting their way through conquest, not trade or collaboration.

In 1519 Cortés took around five hundred soldiers, more than a dozen horses, and a few cannons into battle against the Aztec Empire situated in the middle of Mexico. That year, with the help of some Native allies, he captured the capital city of Tenochtitlán. He did so by allowing smallpox, a European disease, to spread unhindered through the Native population and then attacking the city

Hernán Cortés and his soldiers defeat the Aztecs during the battle at Tenochtitlán. Cortés allowed smallpox to spread among the Native inhabitants before his army attacked.

when the defenders were at their weakest. Ward Churchill writes, "Twelve thousand people, many of them noncombatants, were butchered in a single afternoon, another 40,000 the following day, before Cortés withdrew because he and his men 'could no longer endure the stench of the dead bodies' that lay in the streets."[22] Churchill notes that Cortés openly admitted in his letters that his intention was not simply to subdue the Aztecs but to decimate the entire population of the city, a feat he nearly carried out. One of Cortés's lieutenants, Pedro de Alvarado, conducted a similar campaign against the Mayan civilization just beyond the Aztecs' southern border.

Pizarro conquered the Incas of Peru and Chile with less bloodshed. In 1532, having only 180 soldiers and twenty-seven horses at hand, Pizarro made alliances with several enemies of the Inca and took advantage of a civil war that pitted one Incan faction against another. He overthrew the emperors and subdued the population. He executed the highest ranks of the Incan rulers and tortured those who were thought to know the locations of hidden wealth. Stannard writes, "As in other locales, Indians were flogged, hanged, drowned, dismembered, and set upon by dogs of war as the Spanish and others demanded more gold and silver than the natives were able to supply."[23]

In addition to the rampant murder and executions, European diseases helped level the Incan population. Historians estimate that the preconquest numbers ranged from 9 million to 14 million persons. "Long before the close of the century," Stannard claims, "barely 1,000,000 Peruvians remained alive. A few years more and that fragment was halved again. At least 94 percent of the population was gone—somewhere between 8,500,000 and 13,500,000 people had been destroyed."[24] The devastation the Spanish inflicted on the Native inhabitants of the Caribbean and Central and South America was undeniably massive in its scope. Millions died from the spread of disease, warfare, executions, and enslavement. For some historians, this was the beginning of genocide in the New World.

CHAPTER TWO

Colonial Settlement

Although the Spanish ventured to the New World chiefly in search of wealth, they recognized the importance of adding the land they claimed or conquered to the newly unified Spain. Columbus, after all, immediately seized the islands he touched for Ferdinand and Isabella, and the Spanish who followed realized that—despite the lack of gold—there were crops, wildlife, and other commodities that could be traded in Europe. The other Europeans who voyaged to the New World had similar reasons for making the journey. However, they were also eager to colonize the land as a means of expansion.

The desire for settlement was as much a driving force for the English as was the wealth they hoped to find in the New World. England was confined to its small island, so to grow an empire would require the acquisition of new territory. After hearing of Columbus's discoveries, British investors and the monarchy knew that promise might be fulfilled across the Atlantic. Walter Raleigh established the first colony on Roanoke Island off present-day North Carolina in 1585, two years after his half-brother Humphrey Gilbert had touched modern-day Newfoundland and sailed south along the coast without finding a suitable place to settle. The charter that Raleigh had obtained from Queen Elizabeth I required that he establish a settlement within seven years or forfeit his right to rule over and profit from a New World colony. Lacking support and supplies, Raleigh's settlement ultimately failed, and Raleigh was diverted from his mission by war with Spain and his imprisonment by the queen for an unsanctioned marriage.

English Colonization Efforts in North America

Roughly two decades later, in 1607, England would acquire its first permanent colony at Jamestown, in present-day Virginia—part of the same territory Raleigh had claimed on his expedition.

Like the Roanoke settlers, the Jamestown colonists did not thrive in their new homes. Many did not know how to raise crops or live off the land, and some were focused solely on finding gold. Over time, 80 percent of them died from disease, malnutrition, and other scourges. Those who remained alive did so with the help of the thirty or more Powhatan Indian tribes that were largely hospitable toward the English. Kirkpatrick Sale argues, "That the colony survived at all in its first three years is remarkable due in part to the tenacity of [its leaders], the determination of the investors in London, and most of all—ironically—the supplies of corn provided regularly (given, bartered, or stolen) from the Powhatans' fields."[25] Chief Wahunsonacock, who became known to the English simply as Powhatan, was suspicious of the English because he had some experience with Spanish explorers who had passed through the region from Florida. When the colonists began stealing the tribe's corn, Powhatan turned against the foreigners, and warfare ensued for many years.

The colonists' treatment of the Native Americans was similar to that of the Spanish, but the English turned the Powhatans into enemies only when the chiefs failed to acknowledge King James I as their ruler, the Christian God as their deity, and their responsibility to provide food, animal skins, and willing workers as tribute to the settlers. To force the chiefs to give in to these demands, the English seized what crops they wanted and captured chiefs and their families in order to indoctrinate them in European customs. The colonists hoped that by teaching the Native leaders English ways and manners, the rest of the tribe would learn to become—in their view—more civilized as well as pacified. Because Sale maintains that it was logical for the Indians to resist such demands, he believes the colonists' actions were "nothing short of a declaration of war."[26]

> "That the [Jamestown] colony survived at all in its first three years is remarkable due in part to the tenacity of [its leaders], the determination of the investors in London, and most of all—ironically—the supplies of corn provided regularly (given, bartered, or stolen) from the Powhatans' fields."[25]
>
> —Author Kirkpatrick Sale

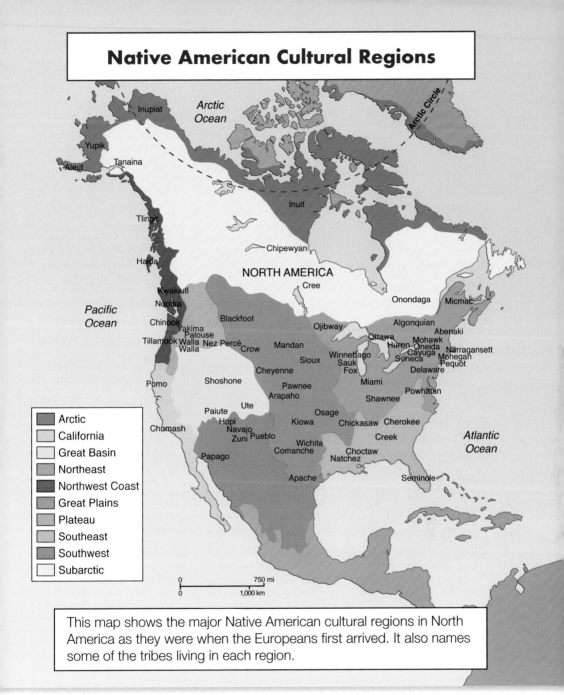

Native American Cultural Regions

Arctic Ocean

Arctic Circle

Inupiat

Yupik

Aleut

Tanaina

Tlingit

Haida

Inuit

Chipewyan

NORTH AMERICA

Cree

Onondaga

Micmac

Kwakiutl

Nootka

Chinook

Blackfoot

Ojibway

Algonquian

Abenaki

Pacific Ocean

Yakima

Palouse

Tillamook Walla Nez Percé

Walla

Crow

Mandan

Ottawa

Huron Oneida

Mohawk

Cayuga

Seneca

Narragansett

Mohegan

Pequot

Sioux

Winnebago

Sauk

Fox

Delaware

Cheyenne

Pomo

Shoshone

Pawnee

Arapaho

Miami

Shawnee

Powhatan

Paiute

Ute

Osage

Chumash

Hopi

Navajo

Zuni Pueblo

Kiowa

Chickasaw Cherokee

Creek

Atlantic Ocean

Papago

Wichita

Comanche

Choctaw

Natchez

Apache

Seminole

Legend:

- Arctic
- California
- Great Basin
- Northeast
- Northwest Coast
- Great Plains
- Plateau
- Southeast
- Southwest
- Subarctic

0 ____ 750 mi
0 ____ 1,000 km

This map shows the major Native American cultural regions in North America as they were when the Europeans first arrived. It also names some of the tribes living in each region.

Justifications for War

Certainly both sides understood that war was inevitable. Powhatan could not peaceably stop the colonists' attempts to expand their colonies into tribal lands. He was also greatly angered by the continuing efforts on the part of the English to convert the Native people to Christianity. The English, on the other hand, believed the New World was a New Canaan—an unspoiled holy land where Protestantism could grow and shape a new society. While some of the English initially believed the Powhatans were innocents awaiting conversion, most considered them savages who worshipped the devil. John Smith, the military leader of Jamestown, referred to the Indians as crafty and deceitful, and according to David E. Stannard, he treated them like the Catholic resisters who had to be brought under control in Ireland.

History professor J. Frederick Fausz maintains that the recent experience with subjugating Catholics in Europe influenced how the Protestants in Jamestown dealt with the Indians. Believing the Indians were obstacles to the rightful dominance of the Protestant faith allowed the English settlers to crush any resistance or respond to any perceived slight with religious zeal. Fausz explains that the English response was often brutal but, in their minds, justified as a means to eradicate a "satanic evil." He writes, "In England's first Indian war between 1609–1614, [the settlers] became crusaders for religious conformity in a Chesapeake 'Canaan,' sparing neither infants nor the infirm as they burned Powhatan villages, murdered native priests, assassinated chiefs, looted temples, conquered tribal territories, and starved a once-thriving population through harvest-time 'feed fights' [battles over crop rights]."[27]

The first significant action in the war with the Powhatans occurred in 1610 when Governor Thomas West ordered a raid on them for failing to return some English runaways who sought shelter with the tribe. The English soldiers from Jamestown burned down a Native village, killed more than a dozen Indians outright, and executed some who were taken as captives. Several ambushes and raids from both sides took place over the next few years, until peace was declared. Yet that peace did not last. In 1622, having now lost much of the tribe's territory to English settlement, Powhatan attacked in hopes of stopping further colonization. The British lost a third of their settlers in what has become known as the Indian Massacre of 1622. Edward Waterhouse, a chronicler of the event, described how the threat was perceived and what reprisals the English could justifiably take. In his *A Declaration of the State of the Colony and Affaires in Virginia*, Waterhouse repeatedly characterizes the Native Americans

The Best Way to Treat the Natives

In "Nova Britannia," published in 1612, a Jamestown settler known only by the initials R.I. describes how the English should treat the Native people with patience and kindness, show them the value of Christianity, and keep the peace so that all might benefit from mutual trust.

> Take their children and traine them up with gentlenesse, teach them our English tongue, and the principles of religion; winne the elder sort by wisdome and discretion, make them equal with your English in case of protection, wealth and habitation, doing justice on such as shall doe them wrong. Weapons of warre are needfull, I grant, but for defence only, and not in this case. If you seeke to gaine this victorie upon them by stratagems of warre, you shall utterly lose it, and never come neere it, but shall make your names odious to all their posteritie. In steed of Iron and steele you must have patience and humanitie to manage their crooked nature to your form of civilitie: for as our proverbe is, Looke how you winne them, so you must weare them: if by way of peace and gentlenesse, then shall you alwaies range them in love to you wards [towards you], and in peace with your English people; and by proceeding in that way, shall open the springs of earthly benefits to them both, and of safetie to your selves.

R.I., "The New Life of Virginea: Declaring the Former Successe and Present Estate of That Plantation Being the Second Part of Nova Britannia," Virtual Jamestown: First Hand Accounts. www.virtualjamestown.org.

as treacherous, barbarous, and inhumane. At one point, drawing on the same religious fervor that fired the colonization project, he called the Powhatans "wicked Infidels" who "despised Gods great mercies."[28]

Waterhouse's book was published by the Virginia Company (the backers of the Jamestown project) and dictated the prevailing attitude that followed the attack. In it, Waterhouse makes clear that, because of the unprovoked attack, the English "as may now by right of Warre [war], and the law of Nations, invade the [Indians'] Country, and destroy them who sought to destroy us. . . . Now their cleared grounds in all their villages (which are situate in the fruitfullest places of the land) shall be inhabited by us."[29]

The Spoils of War

Ward Churchill insists this pattern of colonization was repeated in the Carolinas as well as at the more famous Plymouth Colony of Massachusetts in 1620. He asserts that initially the Pilgrims who founded Plymouth would trade with the Native tribes they encountered and rely on them for food and the techniques of survival in the wilderness. However, "once they'd achieved self-sufficiency, . . . the Pilgrims set about destroying their native saviors with a vengeance."[30] Initially, the targets were the Pequot who lived in what is present-day Connecticut, where subsequent waves of settlers had moved. In 1636 the Pequot leaders took a stand against what they believed was an encroachment on their land. They supposedly murdered a trader (thought to be unscrupulous in his dealings with the Native people) and precipitated a war that lasted a year. With the help of Mohegan and Narragansett warriors, the English burned villages; killed over one thousand men, women, and children; and sold many captives into slavery. The 1638 Treaty of Hartford that ended the war forbade the Pequot from referring to themselves by that name or resettling on lands now appropriated by the English. Both the Narragansett and Mohegan tribes would eventually lose their land to conflict with English settlers, as did numerous other New England Native peoples during King Philip's War (1675–1676)—a war that resulted in the disintegration or dispersal of many tribes.

> "Once they'd achieved self-sufficiency, . . . the Pilgrims set about destroying their native saviors with a vengeance."[30]
>
> —American Indian studies professor Ward Churchill

Churchill and others contend that the wholesale destruction of the tribes and the appropriation of the land on which they lived was an intentional practice on the part of the Europeans who settled in the New World. The colonies of the English and Dutch (who colonized the Hudson River region beginning in 1613) had to expand to make room for the boatloads of new arrivals from the Old World. The Native Americans had what the colonists wanted: land. Therefore, it took little justification to evict the current tenants who, as the pious Europeans believed, stood in the way of the God-given mission to settle this new paradise. Some colonists excused their dreadful actions as a

In an attempt to halt colonization, the Powhatans attacked English settlers in Jamestown, Virginia, in 1622, massacring a third of the population.

form of religious duty. For example, in the wake of the burning of a Pequot village in which numerous women and children were consumed by the flames, Captain John Underhill remarked, "Sometimes the Scripture declareth women and children must perish with their parents."[31] Meanwhile, his compatriot, Captain John Mason, described the bloody aftermath as "the just judgement of God."[32] However, many colonial soldiers needed no religious motivation to engage in the slaughter. As Stannard writes, the large-scale slaughters occurred because "the colonists simply wanted to kill Indians."[33] Their future prosperity largely depended on it, and in the view of historians like Stannard and Churchill, the Europeans looked on the Native people as uncivilized brutes.

The Reduction of the Atlantic Tribes

There are no hard figures for the population of the Native Americans in the fifteen or so tribes that lived in New England prior to European colonization. Conservative estimates hover around 1 million individuals. But according to the New England Anti-Mascot Coalition, a group opposing Native American racial stereotypes in sports, "After 1676 only 4,000 Native Americans remained in southern New England."[34] The population dropped dramatically for several reasons. Many indigenous people were killed in conflicts with settlers and other tribes. Others had been taken as slaves by the colonists or sold into slavery and packed into ships heading to Caribbean markets. Still others were pushed west and north out of the region, with some tribes melding into the Algonquian to the north or the Iroquois to the west. The most destructive factor, though, was disease. Before the settlers came, many of the Atlantic coast tribes had been wracked by smallpox and influenza epidemics brought by European traders and ex-

Natives tend to their sick as depicted in this sixteenth-century engraving. Diseases brought by European traders and explorers proved the deadliest factor in nearly wiping out the Atlantic Coast tribes.

plorers. These biological killers left the tribes with fewer numbers to trade with the colonials or even defend against them.

Scholars such as Churchill believe each of these causes was beneficial to the colonists' agenda of creating a new and profitable paradise in America. Churchill even contends that reports from King Philip's War suggest smallpox may have been deliberately spread through contaminated gifts given to certain tribes. Although no evidence exists to verify that this method of spreading a contagion was successful, letters from Sir Jeffrey Amherst, commander of British forces in the Americas, indicate that in 1763 he toyed with the idea of reducing troublesome Indians in the Ohio River valley by handing over blankets infected with smallpox. Therefore, the British and other Europeans of the seventeenth and eighteenth centuries may not yet have understood the workings of germs, but they certainly knew that diseases could be spread quickly among populations in small, confined areas. Churchill argues that even if the method was untried or proved impractical, its mere contemplation reveals the Europeans' intent to exterminate the Native Americans, not pacify them, convert them, or negotiate with them.

A Difficult Legacy

While some historians believe the attitudes of the European settlers toward the Indian tribes in the Americas shaped actions and policies that were designed to eradicate the Native people from the land, others have a different view. They believe that the Indians were not helpless or blameless in the conflicts that led to their displacement from the newfound colonies. Film historian and conservative commentator Michael Medved claims that savagery existed on both sides of these conflicts. "In fact, reading the history of the relationship between British settlers and Native Americans," Medved states, "it's obvious that the blood-thirsty excesses of one group provoked blood-thirsty excesses from the other, in a cycle that lasted with scant interruption for several hundred years."[35] Medved insists that the white settlers had no clear policy endorsing genocide against the Native Americans and that colonial leaders often urged their people to refrain from fighting with or brutalizing indigenous peoples. Instead, Medved blames disease as the main culprit of decimating the Native populations, and it is clear from his writing that he does not believe the settlers were in any way responsible for the spread of the germs that ultimately killed them.

Author and former political science professor Guenter Lewy supports this argument, asserting that in 1801, after the colonies had formed a nation, President Thomas Jefferson ordered the newly discovered vaccine for smallpox be given to Native people as well as colonists. Lewy contends that the letters from Amherst are an isolated case on which a theory of widespread, disease-based genocide is built, and even the implementation of Amherst's scheme is unproven. Lewy concludes, "The United States did not wage biological warfare against the Indians; neither

King Philip's War

When the Pilgrims founded Plymouth Colony, they enjoyed friendly relations with the Wampanoag tribe that lived on the eastern side of Narragansett Bay. Massasoit, the chief, or *sachem*, at the time, traded with the settlers and helped them survive. In 1662 Massasoit's son, Metacom, became sachem. Known to the English as King Philip, Metacom came to distrust the foreigners primarily for their land grabbing and the growing size of the Massachusetts Bay Colony. In 1675, after an incident in which Wampanoag warriors killed English cattle (probably for ruining Indian cropland), a settler murdered a Wampanoag warrior and set off a conflict that would engulf the region. Some nearby tribes joined with King Philip and attacked frontier settlements. They burned homes and took captives. Initially, the colony's army could not fend off all the attacks, and the Indians were clever at staging ambushes that cut into the soldiers' ranks. The New Englanders, however, did strike back when they could. In the winter, when the Native American warriors slowed their attacks and busied themselves with finding scarce food, a colonial force attacked the Narragansett tribe and massacred five hundred people. Through the spring of 1676, the two sides traded raids, but the superior weaponry of the settlers and the dwindling food stocks of the Indians made the outcome inevitable. After a prominent Wampanoag raiding base was destroyed by colonial attack, the Indian alliance fractured. King Philip was killed in August during an attack on his headquarters near Swansea, Massachusetts, bringing the first great war between the Native Americans and European colonists to a close.

can the large number of deaths as a result of disease be considered the result of a genocidal design."[36]

Medved claims that the argument for genocide is often based on a desire to assign guilt for wrongdoing as a legacy to modern-day Americans. He declares:

> Obviously, the decimation of [the] native population by European germs represents an enormous tragedy, but in no sense does it represent a crime. . . . Sympathy for Native Americans and admiration for their cultures in no way requires a belief in European or American genocide. . . . The notion that unique viciousness to Native Americans represents our "original sin" fails to put European contact with these struggling Stone Age societies in any context whatever, and only serves the purposes of those who want to foster inappropriate guilt, uncertainty and shame in young Americans.[37]

Medved may be correct in asserting that contemporary Americans should not carry the blame for past events that they cannot change. However, those historians who believe the actions of the first colonists constitute genocide might, at least, be calling for a recognition that the condoning of this treatment of indigenous peoples still influences the way in which their descendants are treated today.

CHAPTER THREE

The Expansion West

By the time America asserted its independence from England in 1776, most Native American tribes in the thirteen colonies had been evicted from their ancestral lands. Several tribes had been devastated by disease and conflict with settlers, and their remnants were pushed west of colonial borders. The tribes that stayed in the colonies typically were given land as well as hunting and fishing rights through treaties with England. Often these pieces of land were not part of a tribe's original homelands. Known as manors or reservations, the Native Americans were expected to remain on them, not only to guarantee the safety of the surrounding settlers but also to protect the Indians from harassment from the colonists. Even as the colonies united to proclaim that their territories were their own and not subject to distant rule, they were still hungry to move their borders westward in hopes of enlarging the new nation.

Standing in their way, though, were various Native American tribes that had long resisted the settlers' push westward. Some sided with the British in the American Revolution to keep colonists from moving them farther off their tribal lands in upstate New York. This included four of the six tribes of the Iroquois Confederacy. The British used their new allies to conduct raids on colonial farms and settlements. In November 1778 a group of colonial militia loyal to Britain and a party of Iroquois warriors attacked the settlers of Cherry Valley, New York. They burned homes, killed forty-six people, crushed the faces of corpses with tomahawks and rifle butts, and scalped several of the dead, including women and children. Captain Benjamin Warren, who came on the scene when Continental forces arrived, wrote, "A shocking sight my eyes never beheld before of savage and brutal barbarity."[38] Such eyewitness accounts spread quickly through border settlements and even to the cities along the coast. News of massacres, scalpings, torture, and capture were common, even if there was not always evidence to support these accounts. As Guenter Lewy writes, "Stories of real, exaggerated, and imaginary atrocities spread by word of mouth, in narratives of imprisonment, and by means of provincial newspapers."[39] It was enough, he claims, to have convinced many military leaders to give no quarter to Indians who were suspected of such foul deeds.

Eradicating the Iroquois

In 1779 George Washington, who was then general of the Continental army, ordered General John Sullivan to wage war against the Iroquois. He told Sullivan that his objective was "the total destruction and devastation of their settlements, and the capture of as many prisoners of every age and sex as possible." He said he expected Sullivan to carry out his mission "in the most

Members of the Iroquois Confederacy resisted the Europeans' push westward and began raiding colonial settlements. Soon after, George Washington, general of the Continental Army, waged war against the Iroquois.

effectual manner, that the country may not be merely overrun, but destroyed."[40] It is difficult to know what motivated Washington's tone. Washington believed victory over Britain would come in a decisive battle in the eastern region, so expending men and resources to battle Indians on the western frontier was frustrating. His call to eradicate the Iroquois enemy could have much to do with his desire to solve the crisis in the western frontier as quickly as possible so that the Continentals could get on with the war against the British regulars.

However, David E. Stannard believes Washington's word choice reveals a deep-seated and pervasive attitude that the Native Americans were subhuman. Stannard quotes a 1783 letter to James Duane, a Revolutionary War leader in New York, in which Washington compared the Native warriors who fought against the colonials to wolves, "both being beasts of prey tho' they differ in shape."[41] Yet in the rest of the letter, Washington speaks of the importance of making peace with the Indians so that the settlement of the frontier could continue. He stated, "There is nothing to be obtained by an Indian War but the Soil they live on and this can be had by purchase at less expence [sic], and without that bloodshed, and those distresses which helpless Women and Children are made partakers of in all kinds of disputes with them."[42]

> "There is nothing to be obtained by an Indian War but the Soil they live on and this can be had by purchase at less expence [sic], and without that bloodshed, and those distresses which helpless Women and Children are made partakers of in all kinds of disputes with them."[42]
>
> —General George Washington

Sullivan's mission was so successful that the Iroquois who survived referred to Washington by the nickname "Town Destroyer." Stannard claims that numerous villages of the Mohawk, Onondaga, Seneca, and Cayuga were eradicated to make way for American settlement. There are accounts, too, of colonial soldiers and militia skinning dead Iroquois and committing acts of torture and desecration in retaliation for reports of Native American savagery. In 1784, a year after closing hostilities with the British, the new government of the United States concluded the Treaty of Fort Stanwix with the Iroquois. For siding with the

British, the Iroquois were required to give up their land in the Ohio River valley, a concession that allowed the Pennsylvania territory to grow westward and pushed the Iroquois into Wisconsin and Canada.

The Goal of Expansion

When Thomas Jefferson became the third president of the United States in 1801, one of his chief desires was to see the fledgling nation expand. He organized the Louisiana Purchase in 1803 and sent Meriwether Lewis and William Clark on their famed journey to explore that area and parts westward the following year. One of the goals of the Lewis and Clark Expedition was to befriend Native tribes and secure peaceful trade. Jefferson believed it would be in America's best interest to convince the Indians to cooperate

Meriwether Lewis, William Clark, and their guide Sacagawea explore the lower Columbia River. President Jefferson hoped the expedition would help improve relations with Native tribes and expand trade.

in nation building. However, his motives have fallen under criticism in more recent times. For instance, Jefferson hoped America would remain a land of farmers with a moral center that reflected ties to the soil and small government. In a confidential letter to Congress in 1803, Jefferson spoke of a desire to convert Indians into farmers and raisers of livestock so that they would give up their forests and extensive claims to land and allow more settlement from the eastern states. He argued, "The extensive forests necessary in the hunting life, will then become useless, and they [the Native Americans] will see advantage in exchanging them for the means of improving their farms, and of increasing their

Thomas Jefferson's Views on Native Americans

The Enlightenment, an eighteenth-century philosophical movement based on reason, influenced Thomas Jefferson's opinion of Native Americans. Leonard Sadosky of the Manhattan Institute and Gaye Wilson of the Thomas Jefferson Foundation at Monticello explain that Jefferson's desire to "civilize" the Native Americans was rooted in the Enlightenment theory of environmentalism, which held that people's relationship to the land and climate helped shape their culture, their politics, and even their appearance.

> European naturalists used the theory of "environmentalism" to argue that plants, animals, and the native peoples of America were inferior to that of Europe due to climate and geography. Jefferson refuted these notions in his only book, *Notes on the State of Virginia*, and defended American Indian culture…. "I believe the Indian then to be in body and mind equal to the whiteman," Jefferson wrote. Only their environment needed to be changed to make them fully American in Jefferson's mind. Even though many American Indians lived in villages and many engaged in agriculture, hunting was often still necessary for subsistence. It was this semi-nomadic way of life that led Jefferson and others to consider Indians as "savages." Jefferson believed that if American Indians were made to adopt European-style agriculture and live in European-style towns and villages, then they would quickly "progress" from "savagery" to "civilization" and eventually be equal, in his mind, to white men.

Leonard Sadosky and Gaye Wilson, "American Indians," Monticello.org, 2003. www.monticello.org.

domestic comforts." He then encouraged Congress "to multiply trading houses among them [the Native Americans], and place within their reach those things which will contribute more to their domestic comfort, than the possession of extensive, but uncultivated wilds." The goal, in Jefferson's view, was to get the Indians to recognize the wisdom "in bringing together their and our settlements, and in preparing them ultimately to participate in the benefits of our governments, I trust and believe we are acting for their greatest good."[43]

Jefferson's optimism was evident in some of his personal and public letters. For example, in 1809 when he invited representatives of the Great Lakes tribes (the Ottawa, Shawnee, Chippewa, and others) to Washington for a discussion of peace and goodwill, he wrote of his vision in his welcome letter: "We wish you to live in peace, to increase in numbers, to learn to labor, as we do, and furnish food for your increasing numbers, when the game shall have left you. We wish to see you possessed of property, & protecting it by regular laws. In time you will be as we are; you will become one people with us; your blood will mix with ours; & will spread, with ours, over this great Island."[44]

> "We wish to see you [Native Americans] possessed of property, & protecting it by regular laws. In time you will be as we are; you will become one people with us; your blood will mix with ours; & will spread, with ours, over this great Island."[44]
>
> —President Thomas Jefferson

Yet such optimism was tempered by the reality that many tribes stood in the way of westward expansion and were reluctant to move. In his letter to those Great Lakes chiefs, Jefferson warned, "The tribe which shall begin an unprovoked war against us, we will extirpate from the Earth, or drive to such a distance, as that they shall never again be able to strike us."[45] Stannard believes extirpating, or eradicating, the Native Americans was Jefferson's real plan all along. He argues, "Had these same words been enunciated by a German leader in 1939, and directed at European Jews, they would be engraved in modern memory."[46] Still, in other letters Jefferson wrote concerning the Indian tribes, he always spoke reluctantly about having to destroy Native tribes as the last act of a provoked nation. He frequently restated his desire to bring the Native Americans peacefully into his vision of a nation united.

Jefferson's promise, though, may have rung hollow to the Native populations that had already witnessed the devastation of the Atlantic tribes. Stannard claims, "When the eighteenth century was drawing to its close, less than 5000 native people remained alive in all of eastern Virginia, North Carolina, South Carolina, and Louisiana combined, while in Florida—which alone contained more than 700,000 Indians in 1520—only 2000 survivors could be found." Stannard states that while forced relocation was responsible for a small fraction of the devastation of the tribes, the greatest losses "were the result of massively destructive epidemics and genocidal warfare."[47]

Missions in the American Southwest

Since Florida was not ceded to the United States until 1819, the destruction of Florida's tribes was largely the result of Spanish exploration and warfare. The conquistadors had claimed all present-day Florida and had driven northward from Mexico to acquire much of what is today the American West for the Spanish Crown. Never finding the fabled cities of gold that drove the exploration, the conquistadors continued to kill or enslave the Indians they found resistant to Spain's rule. However, the Spanish could never field enough military strength in the vast area to tame rebellion. Instead, they sent Franciscan missionaries to Texas, the American Southwest, and California to introduce Christianity to the tribes, hoping to bring them under control. Often Spanish soldiers would raid Indian settlements and send back all captive individuals under twenty-five years old to missions for Christian indoctrination.

The missions spread throughout areas ruled by the Caddo, Pueblo, Navajo, Hopi, Apache, Chumash, and other tribes. Ward Churchill argues that the missions were designed to undo Native culture and introduce Indians to the value of the hard work of farming and tending livestock. He paints the missions as "deathmills" where the indigenous people slaved at "arduous agricultural labor" all day long. According to Churchill, untold numbers died in the missions, trying to eke out a living from a landscape that was not suited for raising crops. Even though Churchill says the exact death toll remains unknown, "it is clear that death rates [among Native Americans] consistently outstripped birthrates by as much as 800

Franciscan missionaries conduct a religious service in a California mission. The main purpose of missions, according to some scholars, was to convert Indians to Christianity and diminish their culture.

percent."[48] Hunger and disease were also common at missions, as were raids by roving Indian bands. The missions were difficult to defend, and raiding Apache and Comanche (who were being pushed westward from the Great Plains by American expansion) pillaged and burned several of these isolated outposts. The Mexican government (which had won its independence from Spain in 1821) turned over its land holdings north of the Rio Grande to the United States as part of the treaty that ended the Mexican-American War in 1848. By then, the mission system had ended by being secularized by the Mexican government. Still, the Apache and Comanche kept feuding with settlers in the region, many of whom still lived in and around the missions.

In the Way of Profit

Just days before the United States acquired the American Southwest from Mexico, gold was discovered in California. Where once barely 7,200 Mexicans and various European trappers had lived, the white population of that future state increased to over 100,000 by 1849. Conversely, in 1848, roughly 150,000

Native Americans lived in California; by the end of the California Gold Rush in 1870, barely 30,000 remained. As with other parts of the growing nation, expansion of territory seemed to bring ruin to the indigenous populations. The devastation wreaked on the California tribes was chiefly motivated by a desire for wealth. Seizing tribal lands, murdering Indians, and passing anti-Indian laws were aimed at keeping Native people from interfering with the hunt for gold. As literature teacher Carolyn Lehman writes, "Miners, packers, and settlers ran Indians off their lands,

Driving the Native Americans to Extermination

The *San Francisco Bulletin* posted the following editorial on September 1, 1856. In it the paper discusses the difference between federal policy toward the Indians and local action against perceived Indian threats.

> The policy of the government of the United States when sincerely acted upon and carried out is really benevolent, and the desire of those having the direction of Indian affairs at Washington, is ostensibly to protect the Indians. . . . But while such feelings may influence the authorities at Washington, and even govern the actions of all honest agents of the government who deal directly with the Indians, a very different sort of desires appear to influence a large portion of the inhabitants of our border districts. With them every inconvenience the result of the contact of the two races is to be remedied only by driving the red men back or by their extermination.
>
> We are told that the Indians are treacherous, that it is impossible for white men to live in safety while Indians remain in the neighborhood that the whites are continually exposed to sudden and unexpected outbreaks on the part of the Indians, for which it is impossible to be prepared and fully to run the risk of. Therefore, it is necessary for the whites to rid themselves of the presence of the Indians. If they refuse to move upon the demand of the settlers, a relentless course of punishment for the most trivial offences [sic] is adopted, which is putting into operation without a declaration of war, the policy of extermination.

Clifford E. Trafzer and Joel R. Hyer, eds., *"Exterminate Them": Written Accounts of the Murder, Rape, and Slavery of Native Americans During the California Gold Rush, 1848–1868.* East Lansing: Michigan State University Press, 1999, pp. 49–50.

torched their granaries and broke open fish dams. Indian people starved. Whites shot Indians for sport and revenge, sometimes murdering entire villages. Indian killers proudly displayed bloody scalps and some brought home young women and children as slaves." Lehman describes it simply as "the worst slaughter of native people in American history."[49]

Even before California became a state in 1850, the legislature deprived Indians of the right to vote. Once it became a state, the first governor, Peter Burnett, helped pass the Act for the Government and Protection of Indians, a statute that had nothing to do with protecting Indians. In fact, the law prohibited the conviction of any nonnative person on the testimony of an Indian. It also allowed nonnative people to take any Indian children into custody as wards if they could afford to support them. Such children were often forced into slavery, and their earnings, by law, were turned over to their owners. Even adult Indians who were caught drunk or disorderly could be sold to ranchers willing to pay their fines and then made into indentured servants who had to work to earn their freedom. Since all these policies were a matter of public record, Lehman calls what happened in California a "well-documented genocide."[50]

Not all Californians looked on the Native people as a hindrance to be tamed or removed. In January 1851, for example, an editorial in the *Daily Alta California* newspaper observed:

> [The Indians] are the original possessors of the soil. Here are all the associations of their lives. Here are their traditions. The trees which we cut down are the volumes of their unwritten histories. The mountaintops are their temples the running streams which we turn aside for gold have been the storehouses of their food, their fisheries by us destroyed and their supplies cut off.

> "[During the California Gold Rush] miners, packers, and settlers ran Indians off their lands, torched their granaries and broke open fish dams. Indian people starved. Whites shot Indians for sport and revenge, sometimes murdering entire villages."[49]
>
> —Literature teacher Carolyn Lehman

The wild game, which gave them food we have driven from the valleys, the very graves of their sires have been dug down for the glittering gold which lay beneath. The [recklessness] of our people have not stopped at these inevitable results. They have abused and outraged the confidence and friendship of the trusting Indians, robbed and murdered them without compunction, and, in short, perpetrated all those outrages against humanity, and decency, and justice, which have entailed upon the American public nearly every war which has turned red with Indian blood the green vallies from the Pequod and Narragansett nations, all the way through the continent, which we have taken from them, to the sandbordered homes of the Yumas, and the oaten hills of the Clear Lake tribes.[51]

However, even in such pious defense of the Indians, the editorial elsewhere refers to them condescendingly as "ignorant starving savages" and "poor children of nature."[52] Such attitudes made it easier for all white settlers to treat Native Americans differently, to think of them as beastly and backward, and, throughout America's expansion, to dispossess them of the land because they could not—and in the case of the gold miners—would not be permitted to stand in the way of settlement and profit.

CHAPTER FOUR

Removal, Relocation, and Assimilation

By 1820 most of the land east of the Mississippi River had been divided into its current configuration of states. Only Louisiana, which is in part bisected by the river, held territory on the west bank. Across the river from the states were regions held by Mexico in the south, the United States in the north, and both the United States and Britain in the northwest. Within these vast and varying landscapes numerous Native American tribes already dwelled and others—originally from the eastern side of the river— were pushed.

Figuring out what to do with the Native Americans east of the Mississippi occupied the thoughts of several US presidents. Both George Washington and Thomas Jefferson wished to incorporate the Native tribes into the new nation. Washington, with Jefferson as secretary of state, took office in 1789, two years after the Constitution had given the federal government—not the states—the power to manage affairs with Indian tribes. Both men, therefore, assumed that tribes were equal to foreign nations and had to be dealt with as such. The states found this arrangement troubling because they wanted the land as their own, and it was their citizens who often got caught up in conflicts with the Indians over settlement.

When Jefferson became president, he wanted to assimilate peaceful Native Americans into the agrarian society that he envisioned for the United States. As the Monticello.org website states, "Through treaties and commerce, Jefferson hoped to continue to get Native Americans to adopt European agricultural practices, shift to a sedentary way of life, and free up hunting grounds for further white settlement."[53] However, some historians suspect that Jefferson's attitudes changed over time. Perhaps because of ongoing feuds over land rights and some Native Americans' resistance to the farming lifestyle, Jefferson privately advocated the purchase of Indian lands. In an August 1803 letter to Senator John C. Breckinridge of Kentucky, Jefferson wrote of the territory acquired through the Louisiana Purchase, "The best use we can make of the country for some time, will be to give establishments in it to the Indians on the East side of the [Mississippi], in exchange for their present country."[54] Because of this letter, the idea of removing Native peoples from their lands east of the Mississippi is often attributed to Jefferson, yet he never oversaw any open policy of removal.

The government plan to compel Native Americans east of the river to relocate was instead the project of John C. Calhoun, the secretary of war under President James Monroe. Because tribal lands were considered independent nations, the job of negotiating with Indians was given to the secretary of war, a post that included foreign affairs. In that role, Calhoun devised a policy that Monroe adopted in 1825 to prompt tribes to move westward across the Mississippi in exchange for a guarantee of their sovereignty. By then, he had already initiated forty treaties with various Indian tribes, some of which successfully transplanted eastern Indian tribes across the Mississippi. Perhaps the most well-known negotiations affected the Cherokee of Georgia, Alabama, and Tennessee. Some Cherokee voluntarily moved west when the government promised land and no interference in tribal matters. Others, however, declined to move, causing frustration between both state and federal governments. Between 1827 and 1831 Georgia took the initiative and began appropriating and selling off Cherokee lands to increase white settlement. This caused the Cherokee to petition the US Supreme Court to render a ruling on the subject. The court agreed that Cherokee sovereignty had been violated, but by then a new president had taken office—and he continued to press for removal despite legal judgment.

Andrew Jackson and the Inevitability of Indian Removal

In 1829 Andrew Jackson took office as the seventh US president. His views on Indian affairs were shaped by his previous experi-

The Cherokee were forced westward in the early nineteenth century as the federal government took possession of their homelands in order to increase white settlements.

ence as a general and the hero of the War of 1812, in which he fought the Creek Indians as well as their British allies. He believed the Indians were restless and would continue to be a thorn in the side of the growing nation unless they became citizens and submitted to the laws of the land. In 1817 he wrote President Monroe to argue that the Indian tribes were wards of the United

States, not independent nations, and therefore should be subject to government rule. In the letter, Jackson said plainly, "I have long viewed treaties with the Indians an absurdity not to be reconciled to the principles of our Government."[55]

He believed the government can and should be generous and kind to its wards but not overly indulgent. Most significantly, he maintained that Congress had the right over Indians "to prescribe their bounds at pleasure, and provide for their wants and whenever the safety, interest or defence [sic] of the country should render it necessary for the Government of the United States to occupy and possess any part of the Territory, used by them for hunting, that they have the right to take it and dispose of it."[56] Jackson claimed that the Native Americans east of the Mississippi had more land than they needed. He thought that since most of the game herds had disappeared from these largely settled lands, the Indians could not rely on them for hunting; therefore, the nation had the right to appropriate the unused land even if it had been granted to the tribes. His hope was that Native Americans would simply give up their title to separate reservation land and become, like all other Americans, property holders who were subject to federal law.

Jackson's experience brokering treaties with various tribes after the war, however, proved to him that Native Americans did not want to give up their land. Then again, experience had taught the Indians that the federal government could not be trusted. Knowing that conflicts would continue to occur between whites and Indians if the situation did not change, Jackson became a champion of removing the resistant tribes to beyond the current states' borders. Jackson biographer Robert V. Remini asserts, "General Jackson's commitment to the principle of removal resulted primarily from his concern for the integrity and safety of the American nation. It was not greed or racism that motivated him. He was not intent on genocide."[57] Instead, Remini argues that Jackson

> "General Jackson's commitment to the principle of removal resulted primarily from his concern for the integrity and safety of the American nation. It was not greed or racism that motivated him. He was not intent on genocide."[57]
>
> —Jackson biographer Robert V. Remini

wanted to spare further hostility and possible bloodshed, make everyone in the nation subject to government law, and even preserve the Native people who he knew would likely go extinct—as others before them had—if a peaceful resolution could not be found. However, as president, Jackson's policy in action led to the displacement of several tribes and hardship and death for many of those Native people who were compelled to make the journey west.

Journey to New Lands

In his first message to Congress in 1829, Jackson advocated setting aside land from the Louisiana Purchase to create a re-settlement area for eastern Indians. Congress supported Jackson's plan, and on May 26, 1830, signed the Indian Removal Act into law. The new policy specifically targeted the Cherokee, Chickasaw, Choctaw, Creek (modern-day Muscogee), and Seminole—the southern tribes that had been at the center of the most recent land struggles. The Chickasaw, Choctaw, and some of the Cherokee agreed to move. The Creek and Seminole resisted through conflict; the remaining Cherokee took to the courts to stop removal.

Some of the tribes that made the journey over the next two years were reluctant to submit even as they signed the treaties. Chief George W. Harkins of the Choctaw in Mississippi expressed in a December 1831 open letter to the American people:

> We go forth sorrowful, knowing that wrong has been done. Will you extend to us your sympathizing regards until all traces of disagreeable oppositions are obliterated, and we again shall have confidence in the professions of our white brethren. Here is the land of our progenitors, and here are their bones; they left them as a sacred deposit, and we have been compelled to venerate its trust.[58]

But not all resisted. Choctaw chief Mushulatubbee, for example, saw agreement to relocate as a way to maintain power and standing within the tribe. Mushulatubbee built his strength and support by learning English, trading with whites, and passing out gifts from the Americans to his friends. He likely saw removal

> "We go forth sorrowful, knowing that wrong has been done. Will you extend to us your sympathizing regards until all traces of disagreeable oppositions are obliterated, and we again shall have confidence in the professions of our white brethren."[58]
>
> —Choctaw chief George W. Harkins

as a means of continuing to participate within the emerging market system while keeping his tribe together. Such concessions were on the minds of many chiefs who realized times were changing, the trade in hides and pelts was fading, and dependence on the American economy and government was an unavoidable, if unwelcome, reality.

Those Native people who made the treaty with Jackson's government headed to new land in what is now Oklahoma but was then called simply Indian Territory. The government promised to pay the costs of relocation and compensate individuals for their lost homes. The government also agreed to respect the independence of the new reservations. The Choctaw, who were among the first to make the trek, went in the winter of 1830. Freezing temperatures and dwindling food supplies ended up claiming many lives. While those who made the first journeys were provided with wagons and other conveyances, the government encouraged later travelers to walk in order to save on the cost of transportation. Subsequent waves of Choctaw went in warmer weather but were struck down by cholera. Disease, fatigue, and hunger would mark the journey of every tribe that relocated to Indian Territory. Their lands and homes were immediately snapped up by settlers eager for the eviction.

Trail of Tears

While the arduous process of relocation was different for each tribe and for each wave of travelers, the trauma and hardships ensured that none went smoothly. Because of the suffering and deaths along the way, the Choctaw supposedly called the more than 2,200-mile (3,541-km) land and water route "the trail of tears." That name would more closely be identified with the Cherokee, who during their forced removal from their land in 1838 dubbed it "the trail where they cried."

The Cherokee were the last Native Americans to be driven along the Trail of Tears. Although Jackson oversaw the last treaty

A Soldier Recalls the Trail of Tears

Cherokee narratives of the Trail of Tears are understandably filled with resentment and regret. The following account from Private John G. Burnett, one of the soldiers who escorted the Cherokee westward, gives a white man's perspective of the tragedy.

> The removal of Cherokee Indians from their life long homes in the year of 1838 found me a young man in the prime of life and a Private soldier in the American Army. Being acquainted with many of the Indians and able to fluently speak their language, I was sent as interpreter into the Smoky Mountain Country in May, 1838, and witnessed the execution of the most brutal order in the History of American Warfare. I saw the helpless Cherokees arrested and dragged from their homes, and driven at the bayonet point into the stockades. And in the chill of a drizzling rain on an October morning I saw them loaded like cattle or sheep into six hundred and forty-five wagons and started toward the west. . . .
>
> On the morning of November the 17th we encountered a terrific sleet and snow storm with freezing temperatures and from that day until we reached the end of the fateful journey on March the 26th, 1839, the sufferings of the Cherokees were awful. The trail of the exiles was a trail of death. They had to sleep in the wagons and on the ground without fire. And I have known as many as twenty-two of them to die in one night of pneumonia due to ill treatment, cold, and exposure.

John G. Burnett, "A Soldier Recalls the Trail of Tears," Learn NC. www.learnnc.org.

with the Cherokee that called for their removal, it was his successor, Martin Van Buren, who had to contend with the ordeal. Wanting no further complications, he gave General Winfield Scott the command of seven thousand federal troops to round up and escort the Cherokee westward.

In Georgia, Scott's soldiers hunted down and captured many Cherokee with only the clothes and possessions they carried. Some were taken off the roads; some from their farms; some were found hiding in cabins in the mountains. The army forced about seventeen thousand Cherokee into camps to await departure in groups of roughly one thousand individuals. Some were pushed

Relocation Under the Indian Removal Act of 1830

WISCONSIN TERRITORY

MICHIGAN

NEW YORK

SAUK

IOWA TERRITORY 1832 FOX

UNORGANIZED TERRITORY

PENNSYLVANIA

Mississippi R.

ILLINOIS

OHIO

INDIANA

Arkansas R.

MISSOURI

Ohio R.

Trail of Tears

Mississippi R.

VIRGINIA

KENTUCKY

INDIAN LANDS

TENNESSEE

NORTH CAROLINA

ARKANSAS

New Echota

CHICKASAW 1832

CHEROKEE 1835

SOUTH CAROLINA

TEXAS REPUBLIC (1837–1845)

CHOCTAW 1830

CREEK 1832

GEORGIA

MISSISSIPPI

ALABAMA

Atlantic Ocean

Rio Grande

LOUISIANA

FLORIDA TERRITORY

1832

SEMINOLE

Gulf of Mexico

→ Routes taken by Indians
☐ Land ceded by Indians, with date of cession
☐ Land ceded to Indians

west right away during the heat of summer. Others waited out the hottest months in these detention camps, which allowed disease to spread and take its toll. When these detainees were finally allowed to move, it was near winter. The cold conditions made travel difficult, especially for the old and infirm. Furthermore, because of illnesses within the ranks of travelers, the Cherokee were not permitted to enter settlements along the way, having instead to bypass these places and thus increase their travel time along the 1,200-mile (1,931-km) route. Most Cherokee were on the road or on the water for months and, because of the time stuck in the camps, spent more than a year on the whole journey. According to David E. Stannard, by the time the relocation was complete, eight thousand Cherokee had perished along the trail (though other estimates cut that number by half). He states, "The 'relocation' was nothing less than a death march—a Presidentially ordered death march."[59]

Finally, while the experience of the southern tribes may be the most often referenced relocation story, similar events occurred to northern tribes during Jackson's presidency. Around the Great Lakes, the Potawatomi, Chippewa, and Ottawa turned over a remarkable 5 million acres (2 million ha) of Native land in exchange for $100,000 and reservation space in Iowa and Missouri. As with the Cherokee, in 1838 the last of the resistant Potawatomi were forced off their lands in Indiana by a volunteer army and herded along what historians refer to as the Trail of Death to present-day Kansas. Of the 859 Potawatomi who made the forced journey, 40 died (including many children) along the 660-mile (1,062-km) trail.

> "The 'relocation' was nothing less than a death march—a Presidentially ordered death march."[59]
>
> —American studies professor David E. Stannard

Assimilation

Some Native Americans on the east side of the Mississippi remained there even after the removal policy was put into effect. For example, a few Cherokee fled into the Carolina hills to escape capture, and groups of Potawatomi negotiated with the government to remain in Indiana. Smaller bands of various tribes continued to live throughout the eastern United States in the nineteenth century and beyond. Many of these groups became "civilized" in the view of the government. They raised crops, bred livestock, and, in the case of the southern tribes such as the Cherokee, Choctaw, and Seminole, held black slaves as agricultural laborers. They became assimilated into white culture chiefly through economic necessity and schooling.

Boarding schools for Native children and adults were established in several locations across the country. Perhaps one of the most well-known is the Carlisle Indian School in southern Pennsylvania. Founded in 1879 by Richard Pratt, a military man, the Carlisle Indian School took in Indians from over 140 different tribes during its lifetime. Pratt's plan was to "kill the Indian . . . and save the man"[60] by teaching Native Americans English, converting them to Christianity, and occupying them with a useful trade.

Author Barbara Landis writes that "school life was modeled after military life. Uniforms were issued for the boys, the girls dressed in Victorian-style dresses. Shoes were required, as no moccasins were allowed. . . . No one was allowed to speak their native tongue."[61] Students were not allowed to spend time off with their tribal families but instead were placed with nonnative host families for summer breaks and holidays. Around ten thousand students passed through the academy from 1879 to its close in 1918.

Congress also furthered the policy of assimilation by passing the Dawes Act in 1887. Named after a Massachusetts senator, the act allowed the government to break up tribal land and divide it into lots parceled out to individual owners. The allotment plan mirrored Jacksonian thinking: If the Indians could be made to become land owners instead of tenants on a collectively

Schooling Helps Obliterate Indian Ways

As a young boy, Francis LaFlesche, a member of the Omaha tribe, attended an all-Indian Presbyterian boarding school in Nebraska in the mid-1860s. In a memoir published in 1900, he described how the school eroded Indian identity to force assimilation into white culture. He went on to become the first professional Native American ethnologist after graduating from the George Washington University Law School.

> When we entered the Mission School, we experienced a greater hardship, for there we encountered a rule that prohibited the use of our own language, which rule was rigidly enforced with a hickory rod, so that the new-comer, however socially inclined, was obliged to go about like a little dummy until he had learned to express himself in English. . . .
>
> All the boys in our school were given English names, because their Indian names were difficult for the teachers to pronounce. Besides, the aboriginal names were considered by the missionaries as heathenish, and therefore should be obliterated. No less heathenish in their origin were the English substitutes, but the loss of their original meaning and significance through long usage had rendered them fit to continue as appellations for civilized folk.

Quoted in Maureen Smith, "Forever Changed: Boarding School Narratives of American Indian Identity in the U.S. and Canada," *Indigenous Nations Studies Journal*, Fall 2001, pp. 61, 63.

Students take part in a physics class at the Carlisle Indian School in 1915. Boarding schools were an effective way to "civilize" Native American youths and assimilate them into white culture.

owned reservation, then they would be more like other landholding citizens. The move was also clearly aimed at breaking up the power of tribal governments and giving Washington the right to take whatever land was left over and dispose of it as the federal government saw fit. Several tribes such as the Apache, Arapaho, Cherokee, Choctaw, Fox, Potawatomi, Sac, and Shawnee lost over 15 million acres (6 million ha) in Indian Territory to government purchase. The federal government held on to resource-rich land and opened the rest to nonnative settlement. The allotment strategy did not end until 1934.

History professor Amy E. Canfield asserts, "The goal of the Dawes Act was to terminate traditional Indian cultures, particularly for seasonally migratory tribes, and end communal living."[62]

However, most critics of assimilation contend that this goal could be extended to all "civilizing" missions that followed the viewpoint voiced by Jackson. For Canfield and others, assimilation policies may not have sought the death of indigenous people in the United States (although some argue it may have unintentionally caused more than a few fatalities), but reforming the ways Indians dressed, worked, played, lived, and spoke was a form of cultural genocide. In their view, these policies and actions were designed to eradicate difference and bring "uncivilized" individuals into the proper—meaning American—way of life.

CHAPTER FIVE

The Western Indian Wars

While many citizens and government officials may have wished that conflicts with Native Americans would be eased by forced relocation or assimilation, they recognized that the creation of Indian Territory in 1834 had not brought an end to the troubles. After all, the huge portion of land that originally made up Indian Territory did not remain that size for long. This region initially stretched from the southern border of present-day Oklahoma to the Canadian border in the north and through most of Colorado, Wyoming, and Montana in the west. In the 1840s Iowa and Wisconsin became states, and Minnesota broke away to become its own territory. The federal government had to renegotiate the boundaries of Indian land several times as white settlers moved beyond the confines of the Mississippi River. For example, the Great Lakes tribes—such as the Potawatomi, Chippewa, and Ottawa—had to move almost continuously as new treaties were hammered out. First displaced to Iowa, they were pushed to Kansas and Nebraska and eventually Oklahoma.

The reduction in size meant loss of hunting lands and even prime croplands. For nomadic people like the Comanche or hunters and gatherers like the Sioux, land reductions meant fewer ranges to hunt buffalo or collect fruits and nuts. For all tribes, it meant less land to call their own, a familiar experience for the relocated eastern Indians whose original homelands had been continually shrunk and then appropriated by the government. When gold was found in California, waves of whites rolled and trod through Indian Territory on their way west. Then in 1850, as California joined the Union, it seemed as if white settlement would begin claiming territory from that direction as well, hemming in Native people within an already shrinking region. Fearing more intrusion and loss, some tribes took the offensive. They began waylaying and killing foreigners who crossed into Indian land.

Massacre Sparks Native Resistance

The fear that western settlement would increase and impact Native tribes was realized when gold was struck in California in 1848. The miners' and settlers' murder or eviction of Indians on potential gold-rich territory was appalling, and it was not limited to California. Present-day Colorado experienced the Pikes Peak Gold Rush in 1858. As with the California Gold Rush, settlers and prospectors quickly moved into the area of the southern Rocky Mountains, traveling over lands set aside by treaty to the Cheyenne and Arapaho. Although there was conflict between the tribes and the settlers, a new treaty, signed by some tribal chiefs in 1861, peacefully turned over Native lands to the migrants. However, not all tribes were inclined to make peace with the new-comers. Some bands attacked prospectors and wagon trains that intruded on the land that had been previously established as Native reservations. Seeking retribution and perhaps a reason to evict more Indians, Colonel John Chivington, with the authority of the Colorado territorial governor, raised a volunteer militia that sparred with the hostile tribes in 1864. After a short time, the conflicts petered out, and Chivington met with representatives from the Cheyenne and Arapaho to broker peace.

On the day of the talks, Chivington unexpectedly received an order from his superior, General Samuel Curtis, that stated, "I want no peace till the Indians suffer more."[63] He took about 675 men and stationed them around the Cheyenne and Arapaho encampment at Sand Creek in eastern Colorado. The chiefs, trusting that peace was at hand, raised a white flag over the camp and allowed their warriors to go off hunting. On November 29, 1864, Chivington's forces struck at dawn without warning, killing over 160 Native Americans, mainly women and children. The Sand Creek Massacre became emblematic of the treatment Indians

> "I want no peace till the Indians suffer more."[63]
>
> —General Samuel Curtis

During the Sand Creek Massacre in Colorado, Colonel Chivington's militia attacked a Cheyenne and Arapaho encampment, killing more than 160 Native people, mostly women and children.

would receive even as they sought to negotiate peace. Historian S.L.A. Marshall writes that Chivington "and his raiders demonstrated around Denver, waving their trophies, more than one hundred drying scalps. They were acclaimed as conquering heroes, which was what they had sought mainly."[64] Many Cheyenne and Arapaho warriors headed off into the plains, joining outlaw tribes. Word of the massacre spread quickly among various other tribes of the northern and southern plains, inciting their chiefs to vow resistance to peace by convincing them that the white men would only be satisfied with their destruction.

From Resistance to War

The Sand Creek Massacre was not the first battle in the Indian Wars west of the Mississippi. The Apache, for example, conducted raids against Americans in and around what is now New

Mexico in the late 1840s. At roughly the same time, massacres of Native Americans in the Oregon Territory led to a war between settlers and the Cayuse. However, in the 1860s, at the end of the Civil War, the US military was freed up to engage tribes that rebelled against treaties, tired of seeing their reservation land shrinking and their people being mistreated. Some Native Americans, like Chief Wambditanka (Big Eagle) of the Dakota Sioux, simply continued to resist assimilation of their culture into the dominant American ideal. In an 1894 interview, Big Eagle recalled, "The whites were always trying to make the Indians give up their life and live like white men—go to farming, work hard as they did— and the Indians did not know how to do that, and did not want

John Chivington: Hero or Butcher?

Colonel John Chivington is a controversial figure in the history of the West. He was an outspoken critic of slavery, and as a major in the First Colorado Volunteer Regiment, he became a hero for his action at Glorietta Pass, New Mexico, against Confederate forces in 1862. Toward war's end, he sought a future in Colorado's bid for statehood. His political campaigns were based on ridding the land of Indians. He stood up to those who counseled peace, declaring, "It simply is not possible for Indians to obey or even understand any treaty. I am fully satisfied, gentlemen, that to kill them is the only way we will ever have peace and quiet in Colorado." Taking a position as militia colonel in the burgeoning war against the Cheyenne, he carried out the Sand Creek Massacre, initially earning a hero's parade in Denver for the successful slaughter. However, once news arose of how Chivington's men had butchered women and children, the army began a court-martial investigation for his involvement. But by then, Chivington was out of the army, and no charges were ever filed. The scandal, though, ruined his political career.

Chivington's story illustrates that many westerners were easily convinced that the Indians were a menace that needed to be eradicated. At the same time, it shows that there were limits to the degree of barbarity that the army and the citizens were willing to take in pursuit of that goal. Such attitudes complicate accusations that the settlers or the government sought genocide.

Quoted in New Perspectives on the West, PBS, "John M. Chivington," 2001. www.pbs.org.

to anyway. . . . If the Indians had tried to make the whites live like them, the whites would have resisted, and it was the same way with many Indians."[65]

The conflicts ranged from small raids on settlers' farms or wagon trains to larger battles sometimes involving several nations of warriors. The presence of the US Army and US Cavalry was often defined by the success of Indian attacks. For instance, in the Northwest the army was better established, forcing various tribes to remain on their reservations. In the Southwest the army had fewer forts and longer distances to travel, allowing Apache raids to continue for many years. On the Great Plains, mounted Cheyenne and Comanche moved so swiftly that the US military had difficulty tracking them down after the warriors plundered wagon trains or set farms aflame. In some cases, the army backed down and the government gave in to Indian demands. For example, in 1867 raids by the Oglala Lakota (Sioux) chief Red Cloud were so numerous that travelers along the Bozeman Trail through Wyoming and Montana repeatedly called on the army to act. However, the military, which also suffered from swift attacks that left many soldiers dead, cowered behind three forts built in the region. As the raiding continued, the government sued for peace in 1868, abandoning the forts and recognizing the region as Lakota hunting grounds.

> "The whites were always trying to make the Indians give up their life and live like white men. . . . If the Indians had tried to make the whites live like them, the whites would have resisted, and it was the same way with many Indians."[65]
>
> —Chief Wambditanka

Although Native Americans won many victories in the West, their objectives were defensive: keeping whites from callously intruding on Indian land, ensuring their nations' borders were respected, and maintaining food stocks so that the tribes did not starve. In a meeting with President Ulysses S. Grant in 1870, Chief Red Cloud explained his reasons for going to war against the settlers and soldiers: "The Great Spirit raised both the white man and the Indian. I think he raised the Indian first. He raised me in this land, it belongs to me. The white man was raised over the great waters, and his land is over there. Since they crossed the sea, I have given them room. There are now white people all about me. I have but a small spot of land left. The Great Spirit told me to keep it."[66] No Native chief believed that settlers would be driven from the land west of the Mississippi; 150 years of dealing with European settlement had proved that white settlement was a tide that could not be turned back.

Wars of Extermination

Historians point out that whites embroiled in these conflicts did not have similar objectives. General William Tecumseh Sherman was the Union commander whose devastating march through Georgia during the Civil War notoriously included the burning of civilian homes, the theft or destruction of private belongings, the trampling or burning of crops, and the running off of livestock. When Grant gave Sherman the job of protecting the building of railroads across the West, he brought his strategy of "total war" to bear against resistant Indian tribes that lay in the path. Sherman said that the problem with Indians is that "they did not make allowance for the rapid growth of the white race."[67] Author and economic professor Thomas DiLorenzo claims that Sherman viewed Indians and other nonwhites as racially inferior to Americans of western European stock. He claims that Sherman's own words reveal his belief that the United States must continue to wage war against the Native Americans "till the Indians are all killed or taken to a country where they can be watched."[68]

Later, when Sherman went to war against the Sioux and Cheyenne in 1876, he told President Grant, "We must act with vindictive earnestness against the Sioux, even to their extermination, men, women and children."[69] He gave his subordinates orders to carry out such slaughter and to destroy any livestock the soldiers found. During these campaigns, Sherman also ordered the killing of buffalo in surrounding areas to help starve villages and reduce their ability to make war. Because the Indians preferred hit-and-run tactics and few large-scale battles took place, Sherman's kind of warfare came to dominate the US military strategy.

Philip Sheridan, one of Sherman's able generals, practiced these tactics as well. In the wars against the Plains Indians, he favored attacking Native villages in the winter when the tribes would congregate and food would be scarcest. Sheridan once justified his methods by stating, "If a village is attacked and women and children killed, the responsibility is not with the soldiers but with the people whose crimes necessitated the attack."[70] In November 1868 Lieutenant Colonel George Armstrong Custer, acting under Sheridan's orders, attacked a village of peaceful Cheyenne living within reservation boundaries. Without conducting reconnaissance to find out whether the villagers were friendly, Custer's forces swept in and murdered 103 Cheyenne, including women and children. Though not specifically referring to Custer's actions, David E. Stannard writes that "massacres of this sort were so numerous and routine that recounting them eventually became numbing—and of course, far more carnage of this sort occurred than ever was recorded."[71] However, history does record the massacre at Little Big Horn in June 1876, the event in which Custer's command was annihilated by a combined force of Lakota, Cheyenne, and Arapaho warriors.

> "If a[n Indian] village is attacked and women and children killed, the responsibility is not with the soldiers but with the people whose crimes necessitated the attack."[70]
>
> —General Philip Sheridan

While battling the Sioux and Cheyenne in 1876, General Sherman ordered the killing of buffalo in surrounding areas to cut off a vital resource of the Native Americans and weaken their ability to fight.

The Railroad Speeds the End of the Indian Wars

Officially, the wars against the Indians in the West were in service of some proposed good: keeping Native Americans on reservation land, protecting miners and settlers, or—as Sheridan's first assignment shows—defending railroad workers and railway lines against attack. Railroads were the lifeline to western states and territories. They brought supplies to and promoted settlement in all regions across the vast western half of the United States. The construction of the Transcontinental Railroad (1863–1869) linked the East with the Pacific coast, uniting a nation that was

Native Americans attack a Union Pacific train along the transcontinental line. The completion of the Transcontinental Railroad was a significant factor in ending the Indian Wars in the West.

geographically split in two by the presence of Native American reservations. University of Arkansas history professor Elliott West writes that before the impressive railway could be built, politicians and railroad agents—looking to find the shortest possible routes—had to clear paths through reservation land. "That meant settling up with American Indian tribes and eliminating any of their claims to the country in question,"[72] West states.

The government bought up millions of acres of Indian land to lay tracks. Once those were down, settlements popped up across the empty landscape. West writes, "Every new opportunity for settlers . . . further eroded the dwindling independence of Indians. New towns and spreading ranches and farms pressed against shrinking native homelands, disrupting economies and triggering disputes that almost invariably ended badly for Indians."[73] Along with settlements came forts and depots. These structures allowed the army to move men and munitions quickly, making it easier to wage war against troublesome tribes. Sherman claimed that, more than military campaigns, the railroad had become the most significant factor in bringing about the end of the Indian Wars in the West.

> "New towns and spreading ranches and farms pressed against shrinking native homelands, disrupting economies and triggering disputes that almost invariably ended badly for Indians."[73]
>
> —History professor Elliott West

The Surrender of Body and Mind

The major conflicts of the western Indian Wars ended in 1890 at the northern Lakota reservation at Wounded Knee, South Dakota. There, the US military was disarming Native Americans when, as one account tells it, a rifle accidentally discharged and the soldiers fired into the host of Indians. The Lakota returned fire but were unprepared for a fight, having laid down most of their weapons. An estimated three hundred Native Americans were killed; most of the victims were women, children, and elderly men. The massacres, however, were only part of the explanation of why the Native Americans ultimately surrendered. As the staff of the History website asserts, "In the end . . . military force alone had not destroyed Indian resistance. Only in conjunction with railroad expansion, the destruction of the buffalo, increased numbers of non-Indian settlers, and the determination of successive governments to crush any challenge to their sovereignty had white armies overwhelmed the tribes."[74]

Within three years of the massacre at Wounded Knee, only four hundred buffalo were roaming wild on the western plains. Chief Plenty Coups of the Crow Nation told his biographer in 1928, "[When] the buffalo went away, the hearts of my people fell to the ground. . . . After this, nothing happened. There was little singing anywhere."[75] All but a few renegade Indians stayed on their reservations, some of them slowly adopting the life of ranchers and farmers. Ward Churchill, however, claims much of

An Indian Cavalry Scout's View of the Wounded Knee Massacre

Philip Wells was a Sioux interpreter who served with the Seventh Cavalry, the unit that surrounded and entered the Lakota camp at Wounded Knee in December 1890. The Seventh Cavalry was the same force that had been defeated at Little Big Horn, and some historians contend the unit was eager for revenge. But Wells claims that the soldiers' actions were entirely in self-defense.

> A cavalry sergeant exclaimed, "There goes an Indian with a gun under his blanket!" Forsyth ordered him to take the gun from the Indian, which he did. Whitside then said to me, "Tell the Indians it is necessary that they be searched one at a time." The young warriors paid no attention to what I told them. I heard someone on my left exclaim, "Look out! Look out!" I saw five or six young warriors cast off their blankets and pull guns out from under them and brandish them in the air. One of the warriors shot into the soldiers, who were ordered to fire into the Indians. I looked in the direction of the medicine man. He or some other medicine man approached to within three or four feet of me with a long cheese knife, ground to a sharp point and raised to stab me. He stabbed me during the melee and nearly cut off my nose. I held him off until I could swing my rifle to hit him, which I did. I shot and killed him in self-defense.

Quoted in EyeWitness to History, "Massacre at Wounded Knee, 1890," 1998. www.eyewitnesstohistory.com.

the reservation land was "worthless, unfarmable, arid patches of dust deemed remote enough to allow for the steady die-off of survivors."[76] He believes the surrender and the change in lifestyle were psychologically devastating, leading to depression and a decreased will to live among all surviving tribes. By 1900, he states, the indigenous population in America had shrunk to 2.5 percent of its original size, and the United States had by then appropriated 97.5 percent of the Native Americans' original homelands. Into and throughout the next century, reservation life witnessed high rates of infant mortality, low adult life expectancies, poverty, high unemployment, hunger, substance abuse, and poor medical care. To Churchill and others, these factors—still lingering on Native American land—are no less genocidal than the wars that ultimately broke the spirit of the western tribes.

SOURCE NOTES

Introduction: A Question of Intent

1. Office of the United Nations High Commissioner for Human Rights, "Convention on the Prevention and Punishment of the Crime of Genocide." www.ohchr.org.
2. Roxanne Dunbar-Ortiz, *An Indigenous Peoples' History of the United States*. Boston: Beacon, 2014, p. 9.
3. Rod D. Martin, "Did America Commit Genocide Against the Indians?," RodMartin.org, October 12, 2015. www.rodmartin.org.
4. Ward Churchill, *A Little Matter of Genocide: Holocaust and Denial in the Americas, 1492 to the Present*. San Francisco: City Lights, 1997, p. 86.
5. Kenneth Auchincloss, "When Worlds Collide," *Newsweek*, September 1, 1991.
6. Martin, "Did America Commit Genocide Against the Indians?"
7. Auchincloss, "When Worlds Collide."
8. Dunbar-Ortiz, *An Indigenous Peoples' History of the United States*, p. 2.

Chapter One: The Spanish and "Discovery"

9. Quoted in Gilder Lehrman Institute of American History, "Columbus Reports on His First Voyage, 1493," 2012. www.gilderlehrman.org.
10. Quoted in Gilder Lehrman Institute of American History, "Columbus Reports on His First Voyage, 1493."
11. Quoted in Gilder Lehrman Institute of American History, "Columbus Reports on His First Voyage, 1493."
12. Christopher Columbus, *The Journal of Christopher Columbus (During His First Voyage, 1492–1493)*, ed. Clements R. Markham. Cambridge: Cambridge University Press, 2010, p. 41.
13. Quoted in Gilder Lehrman Institute of American History, "Columbus Reports on His First Voyage, 1493."

14. Quoted in Gilder Lehrman Institute of American History, "Columbus Reports on His First Voyage, 1493."
15. Timothy Foote, "Where Columbus Was Coming From," *Smithsonian*, December 1991.
16. David E. Stannard, *American Holocaust: The Conquest of the New World*. New York: Oxford University Press, 1992, p. 61.
17. Stannard, *American Holocaust*, p. 66.
18. Quoted in Stannard, *American Holocaust*, p. 69.
19. Thom Hartmann, "Columbus Day Celebration? Think Again. . . ," CommonDreams, October 11, 2004. www.commondreams.org.
20. Kirkpatrick Sale, *The Conquest of Paradise: Christopher Columbus and the Columbian Legacy*. New York: Plume, 1991, p. 226.
21. Stannard, *American Holocaust*, p. 74.
22. Churchill, *A Little Matter of Genocide*, p. 98.
23. Stannard, *American Holocaust*, p. 87.
24. Stannard, *American Holocaust*, p. 87.

Chapter Two: Colonial Settlement
25. Sale, *The Conquest of Paradise*, p. 275.
26. Sale, *The Conquest of Paradise*, p. 278.
27. J. Frederick Fausz, "The First Act of Terrorism in English America," History News Network, January 11, 2006. www.historynewsnetwork.org.
28. Edward Waterhouse, *A Declaration of the State of the Colony and Affaires in Virginia*. Ann Arbor, MI: Text Creation Partnership, 2003. http://quod.lib.umich.edu/e/eebo.
29. Quoted in Martha McCartney, "A Declaration of the State of the Colony and Affaires in Virginia (1622)," *Encyclopedia Virginia*, June 4, 2014. www.encyclopediavirginia.org.
30. Churchill, *A Little Matter of Genocide*, p. 148.
31. Quoted in Stannard, *American Holocaust*, p. 114.
32. Quoted in Stannard, *American Holocaust*, p. 114.
33. Stannard, *American Holocaust*, p. 112.
34. New England Anti-Mascot Coalition, "The Abenaki People." www.sanfacon.com.

35. Michael Medved, "Reject the Lie of White 'Genocide' Against Native Americans," Townhall, September 19, 2007. www.town hall.com.

36. Guenter Lewy, "Were American Indians the Victims of Genocide?," History News Network, September 2004. www.history newsnetwork.org.

37. Medved, "Reject the Lie of White 'Genocide' Against Native Americans."

Chapter Three: The Expansion West

38. Quoted in Ron Soodalter, "Massacre & Retribution: The 1779–80 Sullivan Expedition," HistoryNet, July 8, 2011. www .historynet.com.

39. Lewy, "Were American Indians the Victims of Genocide?"

40. Quoted in Soodalter, "Massacre & Retribution."

41. Quoted in Stannard, *American Holocaust*, p. 119.

42. George Washington, "From George Washington to James Duane, 7 September 1783," Founders Online, National Archives. www.founders.archives.gov.

43. Thomas Jefferson, "Jefferson's Confidential Letter to Congress," Monticello.org. www.monticello.org.

44. Thomas Jefferson, "From Thomas Jefferson to Indian Nations, 10 January, 1809," Founders Online, National Archives. www.founders.archives.gov.

45. Jefferson, "From Thomas Jefferson to Indian Nations, 10 January, 1809."

46. Stannard, *American Holocaust*, p. 120.

47. Stannard, *American Holocaust*, p. 121.

48. Churchill, *A Little Matter of Genocide*, p. 142.

49. Carolyn Lehman, "Gold Rush and Genocide: What Are We Telling Children About Our Bloody Past?," *School Library Journal*, September 1998, p. 118.

50. Lehman, "Gold Rush and Genocide," p. 118.

51. Quoted in Clifford E. Trafzer and Joel R. Hyer, eds., *"Exterminate Them": Written Accounts of the Murder, Rape, and Slavery of Native Americans During the California Gold Rush,*

1848–1868. East Lansing: Michigan State University Press, 1999, pp. 37–38.

52. Quoted in Trafzer and Hyer, *"Exterminate Them,"* p. 38.

Chapter Four: Removal, Relocation, and Assimilation

53. Monticello.org, "President Jefferson and the Indian Nations." www.monticello.org.

54. Thomas Jefferson, "Letter to John C. Breckinridge, August 12, 1803," Teaching American History.org. www.teachingame ricanhistory.org.

55. Quoted in Robert V. Remini, *The Legacy of Andrew Jackson: Essays on Democracy, Indian Removal, and Slavery*. Baton Rouge: Louisiana State University, 1988, p. 48.

56. Quoted in Remini, *The Legacy of Andrew Jackson*, p. 48.

57. Remini, *The Legacy of Andrew Jackson*, p. 57.

58. George W. Harkins, "George W. Harkins to the American People—December 1831," University of Arkansas at Little Rock, Sequoyah National Research Center. www.ualrexhi bits.org.

59. Stannard, *American Holocaust*, p. 123.

60. Quoted in History Matters, "'Kill the Indian, and Save the Man': Capt. Richard H. Pratt on the Education of Native Americans." www.historymatters.gmu.edu.

61. Barbara Landis, "Carlisle Indian Industrial School History," Carlisle Indian Industrial School, 1996. http://home.epix.net.

62. Amy E. Canfield, "The 'Civilizing Mission' Revisited: The Impacts of Assimilation on Shoshone-Bannock Women," *Idaho Yesterdays*, Spring/Summer 2010. www.idahoyesterdays.net.

Chapter Five: The Western Indian Wars

63. Quoted in Winter Rabbit, "143rd Anniversary of the Sand Creek Massacre of Nov. 29th, 1864," *Daily Kos* (blog), November 28, 2007. www.dailykos.com.

64. Quoted in Thomas DiLorenzo, "How Lincoln's Army 'Liberated' the Indians," Lew Rockwell.com, February 12, 2003. www.lewrockwell.com.

65. Quoted in Ben Welter, "July 1, 1894: Chief Big Eagle Speaks," *Yesterday's News* (blog), *Minneapolis (MN) Star Tribune*, August 16, 2012. www.startribune.com.

66. Red Cloud, "June 9, 1870: Chief Red Cloud Meets with Ulysses S. Grant at the White House," *The Daily Dose* (blog), Applewood Books. www.awb.com/dailydose.

67. Quoted in DiLorenzo, "How Lincoln's Army 'Liberated' the Indians."

68. Quoted in DiLorenzo, "How Lincoln's Army 'Liberated' the Indians."

69. Quoted in DiLorenzo, "How Lincoln's Army 'Liberated' the Indians."

70. Quoted in New Perspectives on the West, PBS, "Philip Henry Sheridan," 2001. www.pbs.org.

71. Stannard, *American Holocaust*, p. 126.

72. Elliott West, "American Indians and the Transcontinental Railroad," History Now: The Journal of the Gilder Lehrman Institute. www.gilderlehrman.org.

73. West, "American Indians and the Transcontinental Railroad."

74. History, "American-Indian Wars," 2010. www.history.com.

75. Quoted in Adrian Jawort, "Genocide by Other Means: U.S. Army Slaughtered Buffalo in Plains Indian Wars," Indian Country Today, April 10, 2017. https://indiancountrymedianetwork .com.

76. Churchill, *A Little Matter of Genocide*, p. 245.

Books

Gary Clayton Anderson, *Ethnic Cleansing and the Indian: The Crime That Should Haunt America*. Norman: University of Oklahoma Press, 2014.

Dee Brown, *Bury My Heart at Wounded Knee: An Indian History of the American West*. New York: Owl, 2007.

Ward Churchill, *A Little Matter of Genocide: Holocaust and Denial in the Americas, 1492 to the Present*. San Francisco: City Lights, 1997.

Peter Cozzens, *The Earth Is Weeping: The Epic Story of the Indian Wars for the American West*. New York: Knopf, 2016.

Roxanne Dunbar-Ortiz, *An Indigenous Peoples' History of the United States*. Boston: Beacon, 2014.

John Ehle, *Trail of Tears: The Rise and Fall of the Cherokee Nation*. New York: Anchor, 1989.

K. Tsianina Lomawaima et al., eds. *Away from Home: American Indian Boarding School Experiences, 1879–2000*. Phoenix: Heard Museum, 2000.

Benjamin Madley, *An American Genocide: The United States and the California Indian Catastrophe, 1846–1873*. New Haven, CT: Yale University Press, 2017.

Andrés Reséndez, *The Other Slavery: The Uncovered Story of Indian Enslavement in America*. New York: Houghton Mifflin Harcourt, 2016.

Kevin H. Siepel, *Conquistador Voices: The Spanish Conquest of the Americas as Recounted Largely by the Participants*. 2 vols. Angola, NY: Spruce Tree, 2015.

David E. Stannard, *American Holocaust: The Conquest of the New World*. New York: Oxford University Press, 1993.

Periodicals and Internet Sources

J. Frederick Fausz, "The First Act of Terrorism in English America," History News Network, January 11, 2006. www.historynewsnet work.org/article/19085.

Margaret D. Jacobs, "Genocide or Ethnic Cleansing? Are These Our Only Choices?," *Western Historical Quarterly*, November 2016.

Guenter Lewy, "Were American Indians the Victims of Genocide?," History News Network, September 2004. www.historynewsnet work.org/article/7302.

Michael Medved, "Reject the Lie of White 'Genocide' Against Native Americans," Townhall, September 19, 2007. www.townhall .com/columnists/michaelmedved/2007/09/19/reject-the-lie-of -white-genocide-against-native-americans-n989275.

Gilbert Mercier, "Celebrating the Genocide of Native Americans," CounterPunch, November 26, 2014. www.counterpunch.org.

Alexander Nazaryan, "California Slaughter: The State-Sanctioned Genocide of Native Americans," *Newsweek*, August 17, 2016. www.counterpunch.org/2014/11/26/celebrating-the-genocide -of-native-americans/.

Websites

American Indian Genocide Museum (www.aigenom.org). This website offers up-to-date articles on modern events that argue that the legacy of genocide is still impacting Native Americans today. It has links to news as well as blog posts on several topics.

Atrocities Against Native Americans, United to End Genocide (http://endgenocide.org/learn/past-genocides/native-americans). United to End Genocide is an activist website that seeks to spread information on genocidal acts throughout history. Its collection on Native American tragedies includes a broad summary of events related to the devastation suffered by various tribes.

Cherokee Nation (www.cherokee.org). This website devoted to the Cherokee Nation contains a section on the Trail of Tears that details the event and provides some laws and other documents that reveal how the Cherokee felt and how they resisted removal through the courts.

Exploration of North America, History (www.history.com/top ics/exploration/exploration-of-north-america). This interactive site operated by the website of the History TV channel describes the activities of various early explorers and their interaction with the New World. In addition to text, the site offers video summaries of the expeditions of Columbus, Pizarro, and others.

Indians/Native Americans, National Archives (www.archives .gov/research/alic/reference/native-americans.html). Though not all archives on Native people in North America have been digitized, this collection contains some firsthand records of native people as well as pictures and other media. The archive also contains links to various other websites concerning Native American history and culture.

INDEX

Note: Boldface page numbers indicate illustrations.

Act for the Government and Protection of
   Indians (California, 1850), 43
Alabama, 46
allotment plan, 54–55
Alvarado, Pedro de, 22
Amherst, Sir Jeffrey, 31
Apache
   allotment plan, 55
   raids in southwest by, 41, 59–60, 61
Arapaho
   allotment plan, 55
   Battle of Little Big Horn, 63
   gold in Colorado, 58
   resistance after Sand Creek Massacre, 59
assimilation policy
   boarding schools, 53–54
   as consistent failed attempt, 60–61
   as cultural genocide, 56
   Dawes Act, 54–55
Auchincloss, Kenneth, 9, 10
Aztecs, 20–21, **21**

Bahamas, 11, 12
Battle of Little Big Horn (1876), 63
Big Eagle (Wambditanka, Dakota Sioux chief),
   60–61
Bozeman Trail, 61
buffalo, 62, **63,** 66
Burnett, John G., 51
Burnett, Peter, 43

Calhoun, John C., 46
California
   Act for the Government and Protection of
      Indians, 43
   desire for Native American land, 42, 58
   Gold Rush, 42, 57–58
   joined Union, 57
   population, 41–42
Canfield, Amy E., 55
Caribbean islands, 11, 12, 17–18, 19
Carlisle Indian School, 53–54, **55**
Carolinas, colonies in, 23, 28
Casas, Bartolomé de las, 18
Cayuga, 36
Cayuse, 60
Cherokee, **47,** 49
   allotment plan, 55
   escape into Carolina hills, 53
   removal under Indian Removal Act, 50–53

voluntary removal under Monroe, 46
Cheyenne, **8**
   Battle of Little Big Horn, 63
   Custer's attack on reservation, 63
   gold in Colorado, 58
   resistance after Sand Creek Massacre, 59, 61
   total war against, 62–63, **63**
Chickasaw, 49
children, removal of Native American, 43
Chippewa, 53, 57
Chivington, John, 58–59, 60
Choctaw, 49–50, 53, 55
Christianity
   conversion to
      in American boarding schools, 53, 54
      Catholic missionaries, 7, 40–41, **41**
      English attempts, 24, 25–26
      as goal of Columbus, 12, 14
   methods that should be used to show value
      of, to Native Americans, 27
   as motivation for murder of Native
      Americans, 29
   Protestant subjugation of Catholics in
      England, 26
   slavery condoned by, 16
   treatment of Native Americans as in
      opposition to teachings of, 18
Churchill, Ward
   Columbus's extermination of Tainos, 8–9
   condition of much of reservation land given,
      66–67
   conquistadors' intention to decimate Native
      Americans, 21–22
   missions as "deathmills," 40–41
   Pilgrims' relationship with Native Americans,
      28
   spread of smallpox, 31
Clark, William, 37, **37**
colonization
   Dutch, 28
   English
      Carolinas, 28
      Jamestown, 23–27, **29**
      New World as New Canaan, 26
      Plymouth, 28, 32
      Roanoke, 23
   rationale for taking land, 28
Colorado, 58
Columbus, Bartholomew, 19
Columbus, Christopher, **13**
   Caribbean islands claimed by, 11
   early treatment of Tainos, 12–14
   extermination of Taino, 8–9

fate of Native Americans brought to Spain
by, 15–16, 18
motivations for exploration, 11, 14, 16
opinion of Native Americans, 12, 14
slavery proposed by, 17–18
Columbus Day, 15
Comanche, 41, 57, 61
conquistadors, 20–22, **21,** 40
Convention on the Prevention and Punishment
of the Crime of Genocide (1948), 6
Cortés, Hernán, 20–22, **21**
Creek (modern-day Muscogee), 47, 49
Cuba, 11, 12
Curtis, Samuel, 58
Custer, George Armstrong, 63

Daily Alta California (newspaper), 43
Dawes Act (1887), 54–55
*A Declaration of the State of the Colony and
Affaires in Virginia* (Waterhouse), 26–27
DiLorenzo, Thomas, 62
diseases, **30**
introduction and spread of, 19, 20–22,
30–31
as killer of most Native Americans, 10, 40
estimated number of Inca, 22
estimated number on Hispaniola, 19
Europeans did not know germ theory, 7
vaccine given to Native Americans, 32
Duane, James, 36
Dunbar-Ortiz, Roxanne, 6–7, 10

education, 53–54, **55**
Elizabeth I (queen of England), 23
England
colonization by
Carolinas, 28
Jamestown, 23–27, **29**
Plymouth, 28, 32
Roanoke, 23
Protestant subjugation of Catholics in, 26
Enlightenment, 38
environmentalism theory, 38
explorations
Cortés, 20–22, **21**
diseases brought, 30–31
motivations for, 9
conversion to Christianity, 12, 14
economic, 11, 16, 20
Pizarro, 20, 22
See also Columbus, Christopher

Fausz, J. Frederick, 26
Felten, David, 15
Ferdinand (king of Spain), 11, 16
Florida, 40
Foote, Timothy, 15
Fox, 55
Franciscan missionaries, 40–41, **41**

genocide
arguments for, are based on modern desire
to assign guilt, 33
cultural, 56, 67
definition and recognition of, 6
Taino compared to European Jews, 7–9
was intention of white people
colonists, 28, 29
conquistadors, 21–22
if necessary for removal of, 39
punishments for minor offenses, 42
Sand Creek Massacre, 58–59, **59**
spread of smallpox through blankets, 31
"total war" strategy, 62–63, **63**
Washington's order to destroy Iroquois,
35–36
was not intention of white people
displacement was for good of Native
Americans, 48–49
Europeans did not know germ theory, 7
explorers, 11, 12, 14, 16, 20
murder for religious reasons as justified,
26, 28–29
Native Americans were as violent as
Europeans, 31, 34–35
reaction to Sand Creek Massacre, 60
Georgia, 46, 51
Gilbert, Humphrey, 23
Grant, Ulysses S., 62

Harkins, George W. (Choctaw chief), 49
Hartmann, Thom, 19
Hispaniola and Columbus, 11, 12, 17–18, 19

Incas, 22
indentured servants, 43
Indian Massacre (1622), 26
Indian Removal Act (1830), 49, **52**
Indian Territory (Oklahoma), 50, **52,** 57
Indian Wars
Battle of Little Big Horn, 63
destruction of buffalo, 62, **63,** 66
gold discoveries, 58
raiding by Native Americans, 58–61
railroads and, 62, **64,** 64–65
reduction in size of Indian Territory, 54–55,
57
Sand Creek Massacre, 58–59, **59**
"total war" strategy, 62–63, **63**
Wounded Knee Massacre, 65–66
*An Indigenous Peoples' History of the United
States* (Dunbar-Ortiz), 6–7
influenza, 30
intent, as part of definition of genocide, 6
Iroquois Confederacy, 34, 35–37
Isabella (queen of Spain), 11, 18

Jackson, Andrew, 46–49
James I (king of England), 24

Jamestown colony, 23–27, **29**
Jefferson, Thomas
    desire for peace with Native Americans, 39
    Lewis and Clark expedition, 37
    purchase of Indian land, 46
    smallpox vaccine for Native Americans, 32
    views on Native Americans, 38, 45–46
Jewish Holocaust, 6, 8–9

King Philip's War (1675–1676), 28, 32

LaFlesche, Francis, 54
Lakota Sioux
    Battle of Little Big Horn, 63
    defeat of US Army by, 61
    massacre at Wounded Knee, 65–66
land
    allotment plan, 54–55
    claimed by explorers, **13,** 23
    colonists' encroachment on, 27, 28, 32
    colonists' rationale for taking, 28
    condition of much of reservation, 66–67
    discoveries of gold, 42–43, 58
    east of Mississippi River as no longer good
        for hunting, 48
    in environmentalism theory, 38
    Jefferson and purchase of, 46
    Native Americans' relationship to, 43–44
    percent appropriated by US by 1900, 67
    reductions in, allotted to Native Americans,
        57
    taken by warfare, 28, 36–37
    See also removals
Landis, Barbara, 54
Lehman, Carolyn, 42–43
Lewis, Meriwether, 37, **37**
Lewy, Guenter, 32–33, 35
Little Big Horn, Battle of (1876), 63
Louisiana Purchase (1803), 37, 38, 39

Marshall, S.L.A., 59
Martin, Rod D., 7, 9–10
Massasoit (Wampanoag chief), 32
Maya, 22
Medved, Michael, 31–32, 33
Metacom (Wampanoag chief, also known as
    King Philip), 32
Mexican-American War (1846–1848), 41
Mississippi River, tribes removed to west of, 46,
    48, 49
Mohawk, 36
Mohegan, 28
Monroe, James, 46
Mushulatubbee (Choctaw chief), 49–50

Narragansett, 28, 32
Native Americans
    attitudes of explorers to, 12, 14, 20
    attitudes of white settlers to

considered subhuman, 35–36
    as in need of civilizing, 38–39, 43–44,
        45–46, 54–56
    as victims of whites, 43–44
conquistadors' intention to decimate, 21–22
deprived of right to vote, 43
difference between federal policy and local
    actions, 42
effects of slavery on, 20
fate of those brought to Spain by Columbus,
    16, 18
major cultural regions, **25**
population prior to and after arrival of white
    people
    in California after gold rush, 41–42
    on east coast of US, 40
    in New England, 30
    in 1900, 67
relationship to land, 43–44
removal of children from, 43
during Revolutionary War, 34–36, **35**
as sovereign nations, 45, 46, 47–48
treatment of, as in opposition to teachings of
    Christianity, 18
as wards of government, 48
were as violent as Europeans, 31, 34–35
New England Anti-Mascot Coalition, 30
Newfoundland, 23
Notes on the State of Virginia (Jefferson), 38
"Nova Britannia" (R.I.), 27

Onondaga, 36
Order Sons of Italy in America, 15
Oregon Territory, 60
Ottawa, 53, 57
Oviedo y Valdés, Fernández de, 19

Pequot, 28, 29
Pikes Peak Gold Rush, 58
Pilgrims, 28, 32
Pizarro, Francisco, 20, 22
Plenty Coups (Crow Nation chief), 66
Plymouth Colony (Massachusetts), 28, 32
Potawatomi, 53, 55, 57
Powhatans, 24–27, **29**
Pratt, Richard, 53

railroads, 62, **64,** 64–65
Raleigh, Walter, 23
Red Cloud (Oglala Lakota [Sioux] chief), 61–62
religion. *See* Christianity
Remini, Robert V., 48–49
removals
    conditions during journeys west, 50, 51–52
    genocide if necessary for, 39
    Native American response to, 49–50, 58, 59
    to prevent hostilities, 48–49
    as responsible for small fraction of deaths,
        40

routes, **52**
Trail of Death, 53
Trail of Tears, 50–53
of tribes to west of Mississippi River, 46, 48, 49
white settlers' desire for land and, 36–37, 41, 45
reservations, 34, 66–67
Revolutionary War, 34–36, **35**
Roanoke colony, 23

Sac, 55
Sacagawea, **39**
Sadosky, Leonard, 38
Sale, Kirkpatrick, 19–20, 24
Sand Creek Massacre (1864), 58–59, **59**
San Francisco Bulletin (newspaper), 42
Scott, Winfield, 51–53
Seminole, 49, 53
Seneca, 36
Shawnee, 55
Sheridan, Philip, 62–63
Sherman, William Tecumseh, 62, 65
A Short Account of the Destruction of the Indies (Casas), 18
Sioux
    Battle of Little Big Horn, 63
    defeat of US Army by, 61
    effect of land reduction, 57
    massacre at Wounded Knee, 65–66
    total war against, 62–63, **63**
slaves and slavery, **17**
    as common in fifteenth-century Europe, 15–16
    conquistadors and, 40
    effects on Native Americans of, 20
    held by Native Americans, 53
    indenturing of Native Americans, 43
    proposed by Columbus, 17–18
smallpox
    introduction and spread of, 20–22, 30–31
    vaccine given to Native Americans, 32
Smith, John, 26
Spanish Inquisition, 14–15
Stannard, David E.
    causes of most deaths, 40
    Cherokee removal was death march, 52–53
    colonists wished to kill Native Americans, 29
    conquistadors' treatment of Native Americans, 22
    economic motivations for explorations, 16
    effects of slavery on Native Americans, 20
    eradication of Native Americans as Jefferson's true plan, 39
    massacres of Native American women and children by US soldiers, 63
    Native Americans brought to Spain by Columbus, 16
population of Native Americans on east coast, 40
Smith's treatment of Powhatans, 26
violence as part of fifteenth-century European life, 14–15
Washington's order to destroy Iroquois, 35–36
Sullivan, John, 35–36

Tainos
    extermination of, 8–9, 19
    treatment of, by Columbus, 12–14, 18
Tennessee, 46
Tenochtitlán, 20–21, **21**
"Town Destroyer," 36
trade, diseases brought by, 30–31
Trail of Death, 53
Trail of Tears, 50–53
Transcontinental Railroad (1863–1869), **64,** 64–65
Treaty of Fort Stanwix (1784), 36–37
Treaty of Hartford (1638), 28

Underhill, John, 29
United Nations, 6

Van Buren, Martin, 51
violence
    as common in fifteenth-century Europe, 14–15
    Native Americans equaled Europeans in, 31, 34–35
    removals to prevent, 48–49
    See also specific instances of
Virginia Company, 27

Wahunsonacock (chief of Powhatan, known as Powhatan), 24
Wambditanka (Big Eagle, Dakota Sioux chief), 60–61
Wampanoag, 32
Warren, Benjamin, 34
Washington, George, **35,** 35–36, 45
Waterhouse, Edward, 26–27
Wells, Philip, 66
West, Elliott, 65
West, Thomas, 26
westward expansion
    gold in California and, 41–43
    Native Americans as obstacle to, 39
    pushed tribes into other tribes' territories, 36–37, 41, 45
    railroads and, 62, **64,** 64–65
    reduction in size of Indian Territory, 57
    US Army and US Cavalry and
        defeated by Lakota Sioux, 61
        raiding by Native Americans, 58–61
        "total war" strategy, 62–63, **63**
Wilson, Gaye, 38
Wounded Knee Massacre (1890), 65–66

Cover: Depositphotos/adreanalina

4: Shutterstock.com/Anna Nenasheva (top)
4: Shutterstock/Juan Aunion (bottom left)
4: Shutterstock.com/Everett Historical (bottom right)
5: iStockphoto.com/ilbusac (top)
5: Shutterstock/Willierossin (bottom)
8: In the Cheyenne Country, 1896 (gouache on paper), Hauser, John (1858–1913)/Private Collection/David Findlay Jr Fine Art, NYC, USA/Bridgeman Images
13: Italy: Christopher Columbus (1451–1506) claiming the 'New World' for Spain/Pictures from History/Bridgeman Images
17: Spaniards Enslaving the Indians, Book Illustration from Indian Horrors or Massacres of the Red Men, by Henry Davenport Northrop, 1891/Private Collection/J.T. Vintage/Bridgeman Images
21: Hernan Cortes (1485–1547) and his troops during Noche Triste, June 30, 1520, Mexico, detail from Screen with scenes of Spanish conquest, Battle at Tenochtitlan, oil painting by 17th century artist, 213x550 cm, Central America, 16th century, Mexican School, (17th century)/Museo Franz Mayer, Mexico city, Mexico/De Agostini Picture Library/A. Dagli Orti/Bridgeman Images
25: Steve Zmina
29: The massacre of the settlers in 1622, plate VII, from 'America, Part XIII', German edition, 1628 (coloured engraving), Merian, Matthaus, the Elder (1593–1650)/Virginia Historical Society, Richmond, Virginia, USA/Bridgeman Images
30: Prisma/Newscom
35: Iroquois Confederacy, Embleton, Ron (1930–88)/Private Collection/© Look and Learn/Bridgeman Images
37: Lewis & Clark on the Lower Columbia River, 1905 (oil on canvas), Russell, Charles Marion (1865–1926)/Private Collection/Peter Newark American Pictures/Bridgeman Images
41: Spanish Missionaries in California in the 18th century (litho), American School, (19th century)/Private Collection/Peter Newark American Pictures/Bridgeman Images
47: The Cherokee (colour litho), Embleton, Ron (1930–88)/Private Collection/© Look and Learn/Bridgeman Images
52: Katrin Azimi
55: AKG Images/Newscom
59: AKG Images/De Agostini Picture Library
63: Herd of Buffalo (gouache on paper), Baraldi, Severino (b.1930)/Private Collection/© Look and Learn/Bridgeman Images
64: Union Pacific train attacked by Indians. USA./Photo © Tarker/Bridgeman Images